WELLS AND
GREAT WAR

*Based on the lives of the nineteen men
whose names are
on the Roll of Honour in
St Joseph and St Teresa's Church
Chamberlain Street
Wells – before, during and after the war;
and the wartime experiences of their families*

Eric Galvin MA

For all those who fought in the Great War,
their families and descendants,
regardless of nationality, race, gender or allegiance

"… Should we forget their names or story,
'Twould be a stain on Britain's glory."

From 'They Gave Us All'
Frances Mary A. Millard, Wells Somerset,
Wells Journal, 4th February 1922

First published in 2018 by Close Publications
An imprint St Andrew's Press of Wells Ltd
www.standrewspress.co.uk

ISBN 978-1-9996371-9-4

Previous work by Eric Galvin

Eric Galvin (2016)
"Joseph Clark: A popular Victorian Artist and his World"
Portway Publishing
ISBN 978-1-910388-23-5
(Available from the author at eajgalvin@aol.com or Amazon)

CONTENTS

INTRODUCTION

Around the country there are some 100,000 memorials erected by local communities, churches, businesses, military units, local organisations and families honouring people who served in the 1914-1914 War.

Nineteen men associated with the SS Joseph and Teresa Catholic Church in Wells went to war. Who were these nineteen men? The research into them provides strong insights into various aspects of life in the City before, during and after the Great War. The diversity of experiences of the nineteen men reflects aspects of life in many other small English cities and towns for Catholics and the wider population. However, any generalisations based on the lives of the nineteen men are of necessity provisional not least because significant records are yet to be published. The next major release of new information will be the 1921 population census.

It is not a detailed military history, not least because many of inconsistency in reporting from the front line and the loss of many individual records during the Second World War. Some 70% of the 1914-1919 military service records are missing. Even where records survive, they tend to be incomplete making it hard to identify specific individuals. For example, Patrick Kelly appears on the Roll of Honour but which Patrick Kelly? The National Archives have details of around 1,000 men called Patrick Kelly who served in the British Army during the Great War – none of whom have strong links with Somerset. There were probably about 3,000 people called Patrick Kelly serving in the Great War.

After the end of the Great War, the Catholic community in Wells put up a Roll of Honour plaque in SS Joseph and Teresa church listing the men who served in the armed forces. In 2014, burglars stole the original brass memorial. A replacement role of honour will be in place before Armistice Day 2018 based on records held by the Somerset History Centre. The nineteen men were:

> Frederick Chappell,
> Frederick Clark,
> Cyril Davis,
> Martin Foley,
> Ronald Francis,
> William Jay,
> Patrick Kelly,
> Hugh McMahon,
> Bernard Muthu,
> William James Read,
> William Spurle,
> Frederick Trenchard,
> James Trenchard,

Joseph Trenchard,
Joseph Vincent,
Ernest Welsford,
Kenrick Welsford,
William Welsford,
Cuthbert Winslow.

Of these nineteen men, four died during the war and two were incapacitated living on war pensions for the rest of their lives. The nineteen men came from 12 families and had varying degrees of attachment to Wells.

This book looks at the:

Growth of the Wells Catholic Community between 1870 and 1914, a period in which around half of the men on the Roll spent their formative years

Lives of the soldiers before, during and after the Great War

Experience of the Catholic Community on the Home Front during the war. As there are few records or press reports identifying the contribution of individuals, the focus is on the general conditions and opportunities for civilians to support the war effort in Wells.

Events that led from the fighting through armistice agreements to peace treaties – a process completed by the Treaty of Lausanne with Turkey signed on 24 July 1923.

This book uses local records, information held by the Clifton Diocesan Archives, Wells City Archives, the National Archives (TNA), contemporary newspaper reports and from specialist archives held by many institutions. Other information came from web sites including Find My Past, Ancestry, The National Archives Discovery and the British Newspaper Archive.

My particular thanks go to:

Father Philip Thomas, Parish Priest for SS Joseph & Teresa Parish, Wells for his interest and support with the development of this project. The Church is in Chamberlain Street, Wells BA5 2PF and the Parish Office can be contacted on 01749 673183 or at **wells.ssjosephandteresa@parish.cliftondiocese.com**. For further information, see **www.wellscatholics.co.uk**

Members of the congregation who provided their recollections of the families whose men went to war between 1914 and 1919

Julia Wood and volunteers at the Wells City Archives and the Wells and Mendip Museum Library, 8 Cathedral Green, Wells BA5 2UE. To visit the Library call 01749 673477, email: **admin@wellsmuseum**.

org.uk or use the library enquiry form at **https://docs.wixstatic.com/ ugd/1ab9c9_083ba7c2302b4e13a4d7c41f1251082a.pdf** If you wish to visit the Archives, you can do so on Tuesday mornings between 9.30 and 12.00. Please contact the archives before visiting by telephoning Wells Town Hall on 01749 673477 on a Monday afternoon or via the 'City Council contact us page' at **www.wells.gov.uk/index.php?page=contact-us**

Clifton Diocese Archives - Archivist: Rev Canon Dr Anthony Harding and Assistant Archivist: Mrs Gill Hogarth. Any requests for information should be made to Rev. Canon Dr Anthony Harding, Flat D, St John's Flats, South Parade, Bath, BA2 4AF

Mr Steve Wilkinson of the Somerset and Dorset Family History Society, for access to his extensive research on the Hillgrove Estate that housed the sanatorium run by Bernard Muthu's father. The Somerset and Dorset Family History Society's Website: **www.sdfhs.org** and e-mail: **sdfhs@btconnect.com**

Many specialist archives including
    Professor Maurice Whitehead, the Schwarzenbach Research Fellow, Archivum Venerabilis Collegii Anglorum de Urbe, Venerabile Collegio Inglese via di Monserrato 45, 00186 Roma, Italy

    Staff of the Churchill Archives Centre, Churchill College, Cambridge CB3 0DS (phone: (01223) 36087 for information relating to Winston Churchill's entry to Sandhurst

    Rebecca Somerset, Archivist, Jesuits in Britain, 114 Mount Street St, London W1K 3AH (phone 020 7529 4836), **www.jesuit.org.uk/archives-jesuits-britain. Blog: https://www.jesuit.org.uk/blog** for help in tracing aspects of the education, training and early life of the Reverend Father Morton.

    David Knight, Stonyhurst archivist, by kind permission of the Stonyhurst governors.

The extent to which the Wells Journal covered individual soldiers and families differs significantly and this affects the extent to which the lives of the nineteen soldiers and their families can be covered in detail. As an example, Kenrick Welsford who became a City Councillor received over 40,000 words during his lifetime. Others received a few hundred words limited to birth, marriage and death notices and occasional 'newsworthy incidents'. Local newspapers were limited to four pages towards the end of the war and priority went to official notices of various kinds.

In line with tradition, this book writes the words Catholic, Mass and Sisters with capitals when referring to the faith, the celebration of the sacrament of the Eucharist or nuns.

The word 'Roman' is omitted when referring to Catholic Churches in full communion with Rome. The original usage is retained in direct quotations.

There is much confusion between sources about the correct spelling of Frederick Clark's surname. Official documents invariably use 'Clark' whereas the Wells Journal uses 'Clark' and 'Clarke' interchangeably. This book uses 'Clark' except in direct quotations from the Wells Journal.

There is also much confusion about the name of Bernard Muthu's father. His full name was David Jacob Aaron Chowry Muthu. At the request of family members he is called 'David' in this book, apart from direct quotes from the Wells Journal.

The author is available to provide talks about the people, places and issues covered in this book. Contact Eric Galvin by email at eajgalvin@aol.com.

THE CATHOLIC COMMUNITY IN WELLS
BEFORE THE GREAT WAR

The common factor linking the nineteen men on the Roll of Honour is their relationship with the Catholic Church as perceived by the Catholic Community in the 1920s who prepared the original roll of honour. This is not to say that the men necessarily knew each other or had grown up in the city. Before looking at individuals, it makes sense to look at how the Catholic life developed during the formative years of the soldiers born and raised in the city.

Wells before the Great War

The Catholic Community in Wells can be traced to the arrival of a Carmelite convent in 1875. A few years earlier, the National Gazetteer (1868) said that Wells was *'well-paved, lighted with gas, and supplied with water. The town had a literary and scientific institution, a mechanics' institution and an agricultural society. There was a prison, a workhouse, and the county lunatic asylum. In the neighbourhood were several extensive paper and corn mills, several breweries, a brush factory and gasworks. There were lead, iron, and manganese mines but their output was falling. The corn market had decayed, but the market for cheese remained important. The City had three railway stations giving it good access to the rest of the country.'*

According to the population census of 1911, the City's population was 4,655. A century later, the population was 10,536 – an increase of 126%.

The Catholic Community

The modern catholic community in Wells dates from 16th July 1875 when Bishop Clifford of Clifton celebrated the first public Catholic Mass in the city since the reformation. During the 341 years between the the Act of Supremacy (1534) and 1875 there were no formal arrangements to support Catholics living in the city. Bishop Clifford used a small temporary structure on the site of SS Joseph and Teresa's in Chamberlain Street for this Mass.

William Hugh Joseph Clifford (1823–1893) served as Bishop of Clifton from 1857 to 1893. Born in Irnham, Lincolnshire, he was the son of Hugh Clifford, 7th Baron Clifford of Chudleigh and Mary Lucy Weld, daughter of Cardinal Thomas Weld, who become a priest following his wife's death. William Clifford became a priest in 1851, a bishop in 1857 and attended first Vatican Council in 1869-70.

Prior to 1875, the small number of Catholics in Wells could use other local churches that opened in the early part of the nineteenth century. These included Shepton Mallet (1804 – 6 miles), Hinton Blewett (1806 – 9 miles), Downside Abbey (1814 -10 miles); and the chapel at Shortwood.

Extracts from Diocesan archives suggest that there was just over a three-fold increase in the numbers of Catholic adults in Wells between 1870 and 1914.

1870 - 30
1903 - 60
1914 - 115 (98 adults / 17 children and 15 Belgian refugees)
1932 - 168 (including 15 resident at the Somerset Lunatic Asylum)

These is suggests that around 2% of the City's population were Catholics in 1911 with a 50% growth in the decade or so after the armistice.

Catholic Institutions in Wells

Shortly after the first public mass in Juyl 1875, five important Catholic institutions began to emerge. These were:

The Carmelite Convent at 'The Vista' (11 Chamberlain Street) opened in July 1875. It housed about 17 'Sisters' during the nineteenth century. The convent's chaplain served the growing catholic population until the middle of the 20th Century. This was an enclosed order.

St Mary's Convent at 22 Chamberlain Street opposite SS Joseph and Teresa's church opened in 1876 but closed in 1879. It reopened in 1887 and remained until 1936. The Sisters came from the Sisters of the Third Order of St Teresa and played an important role in Catholic Education in the City having strong links with many prominent people in Wells and beyond.

The Church of SS Joseph and Teresa replaced the temporary chapel built in 1875. On 17th October 1877, Bishop Clifford performed the 'Solemn Opening' of the new SS Joseph and Teresa church with a Pontifical High Mass.

The Presbytery where the priest and his housekeeper lived was also in Chamberlain Street. Initially the priest and his housekeeper lived within the convent but subsequently the priests lived in a sequence of 7 different addresses on Chamberlain Street.

The Catholic School built on land acquired at the same time as The Vista, had an entrance on Union Street. It gained certification from the Education Department for 118 children in July 1889 although the 'catholic schoolroom' was already in use as early as 1884. Several of the men listed on the Roll of Honour or their siblings went to this school.

The mansion in Chamberlain Street, known as 'The Vista', had been part of fashionable society in Wells in the 18th Century and served as the 'constituency home' for several of the City's MPs. It went through several changes of ownership and tenancy in the first half of the 19th century.

When 'The Vista' came up for sale in 1874, Bishop Clifford of Clifton saw his chance to solve two pressing problems – the requirement for a new home for a group of Carmelite nuns from Plymouth and for the Catholic community in Wells to have its own church and priest. He suggested that the Sisters might move to Wells. Once the Carmelites accepted the proposal, negotiations to buy The Vista took place in great secrecy because of the fear of strong objections from some in the city and the risk of inflating the purchase price. There may also have been a restrictive clause in the will of the previous owner forbidding the sale of the Vista to Catholics. The agreed purchase price was £2,250 – around £3.65m in 2018 values.

In 1871, there were 11 members of the Carmelite community in Plymouth. In 1875, Reverend Mother Frances Sarah Clayton (b 1833) who had led the community for some years became the Mother Superior of the new convent in Wells and remained so until her death in 1909. By 1881, six of these Sisters from Plymouth were living in Wells together with a number of Sisters in their twenties. This suggests that Wells quickly became an attractive place for young women thinking of following a religious vocation.

On the 4th April 1877, Bishop Clifford visited Wells to celebrate Mass in the Convent's temporary chapel and admit the first two novices to the convent. The novices were Mary Fagg from Canterbury and the Hon. Edith Teresa Clifford, third daughter of the Lord Clifford of Ugbrooke Park in Devon. Bishop Clifford was her uncle. The Wells Journal made a point of reporting that many Protestants attended the service suggesting that any opposition to the new catholic convent had been short lived.

By 1881, the main Carmelite convent had 17 Sisters. Their occupation, as described on that year's census return, was *'Prayer and Active Works, Nun'*.

An entry in the 1891 Census suggests that the convent may have provided temporary accommodation for visitors. In that year, residents in the Convent included Beatrice L Meyer (b 1853) a single woman described as an 'Artist Sculptor Portrait Painter'. She was a well-known artist exhibiting between 1880 and 1900 at the the Institute of Painters in Watercolours, Society of British Artists and the Royal Academy. She specialised in historical scenes, many featuring royalty. Later, she moved to live in Yarley and then Tor Street, Wells before her death in Hammersmith in 1916.

The artistic aspect of the convent's guests resurfaced in 1936 when the Journal reported,

"Miss Doreen Smith, the novelist, who became a Catholic in 1927 after being trained in an Anglican missionary college, has entered the Carmelite Convent at Wells as a postulant. Miss Smith wrote four novels —Quest, East Wind, Lonely Traveller and The Gates are Open. The last named was published just before she entered the convent a fortnight ago. She was born at Clifton, Bristol, and educated at Clifton High School."

In 1972, the Carmelite Sisters left Wells and moved to the order's convent in Darlington. On Chamberlain Street, the Vista building became apartments. The Sister's choir became the transept and parts of the house became part of the church. Parts of the convent grounds formed a new church entrance and the remainder of the garden, maintained by Frederick Trenchard in the Edwardian period, provided land for new housing called the 'Old Convent Garden'.

St Mary's Convent

In 2011, Mrs Gill Hogarth (Assistant Archivist, Diocese of Clifton) delivered a paper at SS Joseph and Teresa Catholic Parish for the English Catholic History Association on 'Persecution and Perseverance, Survival of Catholicism in Somerset'.

She noted, *"The Sisters of the Third Order of St Teresa came from Wardour [near Salisbury] to Wells in 1876, with the intention of running the mission school. They left three years later, but returned in 1887 when Bishop Clifford purchased No 22, Chamberlain Street for them. Some five or six nuns managed to eke out a precarious existence teaching at the school, but the Order left finally in 1936."*

Their convent, known as St Mary's, was heavily engaged with the Catholic school with one of its nuns being the head teacher in the late nineteenth century. The number of Sisters remained constant and various aspects of their service to the community appeared from time to time in the Wells Journal over many years. They played an important role in supporting the Catholic school and contributing to many public causes in the City. Doubtless, there were many aspects of the comfort and support they provided to local people went unreported. One of the more unusual donations from the Convent came in 1932 when new workshops opened for unemployed workers in Union Street. The Journal reported that *'An anthracite stove has been given by the Rev. Mother Prioress, of the Carmelite Convent'*.

One of the nuns who arrived in 1876 at the age of 25 was Miss Charlotte Louise Stones, otherwise known as Sister and then Reverend Mother Mary Joseph. She was a teacher and then head teacher at the Catholic school. She moved on to become a School Manager (equivalent to a 21st century School Governor) and in this role attended many events for the children at the school, often presenting gifts of books, toys and sweets.

In her role as the Reverend Mother, she was well known and connected with many prominent local families. During her time as the head of the community, she gave regularly to local fund raising collections including the Hospital Endowment Fund marking Queen Victoria's Diamond Jubilee (1897), Belgian Pound Day (1916) and the War Memorial Fund (1922); displayed flags and bunting for national occasions; attended many funerals and weddings of members of prominent families in Wells.

When the convent closed in 1935, she moved with two other elderly Sisters to Stroud but returned to Wells soon afterwards. She died in 1936 at the age of 85. Three of the Catholics remembered on the Roll of Honour attended her funeral – Frederick Clark, and James and Kenrick Welsford.

Church of SS Joseph and Teresa

The third Catholic institution with its origins in the 1870s is the Church of SS Joseph and Teresa – patrons of the two convents. The Reverend Francis Gatti was the first Priest in Charge in Wells.

Within two years of Bishop Clifford's initiative, Mr John Mercer of Wigan, the nephew of one of the Sisters, undertook to provide the money to build a permanent chapel in the convent grounds, for the benefit of both the Sisters and other Catholics in Wells.

In early March 1877, the City's Surveyor submitted draft plans to the City Council. The exterior resembled the Slipper Chapel in the pilgrimage village of Walsingham, 5 miles from Wells–next–the–Sea in Norfolk while the wooden barrel roof reflected those found in many Pre-Reformation Somerset churches. The plans were approved by the Council at the end of March *'subject to replacing the iron railings in front of the Vista, so as to form a straight line from the west pillar of the main entrance gate of the Vista to the east end of the railings in front of Dr Livett's houses'*. The architect was Charles Hansom and the contractors were Messrs. F. and Q. Brown, of Frome.

Charles Francis Hansom (1817 – 1888) was born into a Catholic family in York. He was the brother of Joseph Aloysius Hansom, architect and creator of the Hansom cab. In 1859, Charles established an independent architectural practice in Bath with his son Edward as an articled clerk. By the 1870s, this became a large West Country practice specialising in church and collegiate work with its offices in Bristol.
Bishop Clifford blessed and laid the Corner Stone on 19th March 1877, the feast of St, Joseph. The Reverend Fathers A. Kyan (chaplain to the Convent), A. Russell (Clifton) and E. Arundell and F. Fanning (Shepton Mallet) assisted the Bishop. The chapel was dedicated to *'the honour of Almighty God, 'under the invocation of St. Joseph and St. Teresa'*. The Reverend E Arundell was Everard Aloysius Gonzaga Arundell (1834 – 1907) was the priest at Shepton Mallet in 1881. In 1906, he became the 13th Baron Arundell of Wardour, a year before he died.

The church, essentially today's nave, opened on 15th October 1877. After the Pontifical High Mass, about eighty guests celebrated with a luncheon at the Swan Hotel. In 1888, the current sanctuary was added. Canon Alexander Scoles, a noted architect and priest, designed a handsome altar and reredos for Wells. There was a new choir for the Sisters leading off to the left, behind a solid wall with a grille, shielding the Sisters from public view. A former altar boy from the 1950s recalls that the grill had a number of 'letter box' like openings through which the host was placed on the nuns' tongues.

This, in essence, was the church attended by the men listed on the Roll of Honour both before the Great War and subsequently until the Carmelite Convent closed in 1972.

The stained glass in the east window (depicting Our Lady of Mount Carmel with four saints) dates from 1925. Another stained glass window in the south nave wall depicts the Nativity and the Crucifixion. In the 1970s, the nuns' choir became the transept with a large arch formed into the sanctuary, a sacristy and porch. Bishop Alexander blessed and opened these additions to the church on 19 March 1975.

Presbytery

Father Philip Thomas has been the Parish Priest since 2008 and is the 29th priest since the Rev Francis Gatti arrived in 1875. The convent chaplain and parish priests have lived in the Convent and at least seven other properties on Chamberlain Street.

- In 1880, Vista Cottage was built next to the Convent for the Chaplain
- From 1883, 1 Chamberlain Street was used
- Then in 1901 the Census shows Father Chandler residing at 11 Chamberlain Street (the Carmelite Convent)
- Between 1911 and 1918, the priests lived at 14 Chamberlain Street
- Between 1918 and 1925, the presbytery was at 4 Chamberlain Street
- Between 1925 and 1965, the priest lived at 5 Chamberlain Street
- Since 1965, the presbytery has been at 16 Chamberlain Street.

In the nineteenth and early twentieth centauries, Catholic priests usually had a resident servant or housekeeper. Wells was no exception. In 1881, Josephine Trenchard (b 1864) – sister to one of the men on the Roll of Honour and aunt to three others – lived in Vista Cottage as a servant to Father Frederick Neve. Ten years later, her older sister, Elizabeth Trenchard (b 1861) was a servant to Father John Berard at 1 Chamberlain Street. Subsequently, she spent almost 30 years as housekeeper for Rev. Father Carroll moving with him as his career took him to Bristol, East Harptree and Shepton Mallet. She died aged 73 on Christmas Day 1937 at her nephew's (James Trenchard) home in Wells.

Catholic School

The creation of a Catholic school was one of Bishop Clifford's main ambitions in 1875. Its opening meant that Wells had a full range of support for Catholic families in the area. There were several references in the Wells Journal to the Catholic School Room on Union Street. It is not clear whether this was a full school, not least because in 1877 a case before the Borough Magistrates involving the failure of 12 parents to send their children to school. Some of the defendants pleaded that their children had been ill, but could produce no certificate to that effect, and others stated that they sent their children to the Catholic school. The magistrates decided that the Catholic school was not a 'registered elementary school', and all the defendants (with the exception of one who satisfied the Bench that his child had been ill), were fined 5s each (around £22 in 2018 values) including costs.

Later in 1889, the Borough Special Sessions received a school attendance committee report stating that the Education Department had certified the Catholic school for 118 children. At the time, the estimated number of children in Wells subject to the Education Act was about 1,000. It is unclear whether this was a newly registered school or the renewal of a previous registration. The school attendance committee was part of the 'Board of Guardians' whose other duties included poor law relief and running the 'Workhouse'. During the debate in the City Council, one member pointed out that the City's byelaws appeared to say that young people were at liberty to leave school at 13 years of age, whereas the 1870 Education Act said they must not do so until they had attained the age of 14. The Council resolved that the byelaws should be revised and made in harmony with the Education Act.

In 1897, 84 students from the Catholic School took part in the procession to mark Queen Victoria's Golden Jubilee. In 1911, 62 students from the Catholic School took part in the Coronation procession in the City supervised by four teachers - Misses Buckley, Vaughan, Cox, and Trenchard. This is somewhat surprising as in later years, one of the Miss Buckleys was a committed supporter of the Irish Republican cause. Children of the Catholic School, under the other Miss Buckley, by that time Mrs. Evens took part in the Peace Day processions in July 1919.

The position of the churches and of religious instruction in schools was a complex and difficult issue facing the Board of Guardians after the Elementary Education Act 1870 and the five further Education Acts over the following two decades. At various stages, the Catholic Church nationally was involved in large scale campaigning and lobbying to protect the position of Catholic Schools – sometimes in partnership with Anglican and Free Church Schools. Reverend Mother Mary Joseph played an active role in these campaigns, as did Father Morton, who became the priest-in-charge in 1914.

In 1906, Father Chandler became the Catholic School's representative on the newly established Wells Education Committee under Section 17 of the Education Act, 1902. In 1907, E. A. Crosse joined the committee representing the Catholic School. He lived on Chamberlain Street but was not himself a Catholic. He held this position until after the Great War.

Several aspects of school life during the decades when some of the men on the Roll of Honour who attended the Catholic School tell us something about the education they received. One was scholarships to meet some of the costs of able pupils from poor homes progressing to the Blue Schools or the Wells Grammar School. By 1889 young people attending all Elementary Schools within three miles of Wells were eligible to compete for a scholarship to the Blue Schools if they had reached a sufficiently high level of educational attainment at their current school.

Not many achieved these scholarships and the records are patchy. In 1908, the Journal reported that '*Miss Stella Elfreda Maud Coggan of No 1 Ethel-street (pupil at the Roman Catholic School Wells), has taken the first prize in the cookery class, held under the auspices of the Board of Education'*. In 1909, when Ena Coggan and James Hugh MacMahon both secured entrance scholarships for the Blue School. They both took important roles in the annual 'entertainments' staged by the Catholic school as did members of several other families whose sons went to war including the Trenchards and Welsfords. In 1912, Georgina Stevens of the Catholic School secured a scholarship to the Blue School.

In 1910, Ena took part in an 'acclaimed entertainment' by the St Cuthbert's branch of the Band of Hope. In May 1911, she achieved an intermediate award for piano at an examination in connection with London College of Music. By 1915, she was described as a '*pupil at the Girls' High School, Wigan, and formerly of the Girls' Blue School, Wells,' when she passed the Oxford Senior Examination.'*

In 1926, she married James Hugh MacMahon one of the men on the Roll of Honour. They lived in Worle and he was a stationmaster for the Great Western Railway at the time of the 1939 Register. He died in Wells in 1985 aged 86 and she died aged 96 in Weymouth in 1993. Another important aspect of school life was the relationship with the Board of Guardians. They employed the School Attendance Officers who reported regularly on numbers of pupils and the proportions attending school. In 1893, the Catholic school had 84 pupils and an attendance rate of 81% - the lowest in the city. By summer 1895, there were 80 pupils and an attendance rate of 90%. In 1897, Catholic School had 80 pupils and a 66% attendance rate. Attendance rates were seasonal, partly because some children worked on farms helping with the harvest.

Another aspect of these seasonal fluctuations was the health of pupils. In 1894, the Catholic School was affected by the outbreak of Scarlet fever. The Medical officer of Health served the 'usual formal notices' and supplied disinfectants to the parents. By the request of the Medical Officer, the Rev. Mother in charge of the Catholic schools had the school thoroughly fumigated with sulphur. In 1897, the Medical Officer of Health visited all the schools in the city to offer advice on precautions to beat an outbreak of typhoid in the City.

In 1896, the Journal reported, "*The Inspector of Nuisances* (another official of the Board of Guardians) *reported that on the 10th May he visited a case of typhoid fever at 32 South*

Street, the patient being a girl of 17 years of age. By order of the Medical Officer, the patient was removed to the Sanitary Hospital. Everything in the house was remarkably clean, but it was small, and without any back-let. The Inspector also reported that he had visited the Catholic Schools, the Central Schools, Blue Schools, St. Thomas' Schools, and the Grammar School, and found all the sanitary arrangements clean and in good order."

In July 1908, the Journal reported, *"Owing to the epidemic of measles, it has been deemed inadvisable to allow the children of the Central and Roman Catholic schools to reassemble yet, and it has therefore been decided not to re-open until after the conclusion of the summer holiday, namely August 31st."* In October 1909, the Medical Officer recommended that the Catholic Schools should remain closed *'because of the prevalence of mumps'*.

The school also contributed to several important national celebrations alongside other schools in the city. These included processions to mark Queen Victoria's Diamond Jubilee in 1897, the coronations of King Edward VII (1902) and King George V (1911) and Peace Day (July 1919).

Each year it also offered a well-received annual 'entertainment' for parents and friends of the school. Most entertainments offered a mix of songs and short plays. The cast lists provide insights into who went to the school and those who contributed to such events. This shows the extent to which the school was instrumental in building links between the leading Catholic families including those whose sons went to war after 1914. Reports of these entertainments in the Journal continue until the 1930s, by which time the second and third generations of the same families were participating.

As with Ena Coggan and James Hugh MacMahon, the relationships formed at school continued into adult life resulting in several marriages amongst the 'war generation' of Catholics.

The church, the two convents and the school provided a nurturing and supportive framework of Catholic institutions within which some of the young men on the roll of honour grew up. As we will see later, several of the young men on the Roll spent some of their formative lives elsewhere and moved to Wells before the war.

What did it mean to be a Catholic in the early 20th Century?

A young person born into a Catholic family in the 1890s would have received several sacraments before reaching adulthood, starting with baptism as a baby. By the age of seven or eight' they would have made their 'First Confession' (the sacrament of 'Penitence') and Holy Communion. Later, around 13, they were confirmed in their faith. As adults, they may have received the sacraments of marriage and anointing the sick.

As well as receiving these sacraments, Catholics were expected to attend Mass every Sunday and on the great feasts of the Church including Epiphany of the Lord (6th

January), Saints Peter and Paul, (29th June), Assumption of the Blessed Virgin Mary (15th August), All Saints (1st November), Immaculate Conception of the Blessed Virgin Mary (8th December) and Christmas (25th December).

Four further holy days of obligation are determined by the date of Easter Sunday. This is 'the first Sunday after the full moon following the first day of spring – normally between 22nd March and 25th April'. As well as Easter Sunday itself, there are three associated holy days of obligation; Ash Wednesday (40 days before Easter Sunday), Good Friday (the Friday immediately before Easter) and Ascension Day (Thursday of the sixth week of Eastertide). Catholics of this generation were encouraged to make Penitence weekly, often on Saturday afternoons, and take the Eucharist at least once a week.

The depth of feeling created by these obligations for some of the congregation can be seen clearly in a press report of a case in the City's Police Court from 1917. The defendant was the mother and stepmother respectively of two of the men on the Roll of Honour.

The Wells Journal reported: *"Elizabeth Francis, 45, a widow, described as a road contractor, of Hembry Wood, Wookey, and her son, John Spurle, 16, labourer, of the same place, were charged jointly with stealing 31 lbs. of hay from a rick at Corps Mead, Wookey, value Is. 6d., the property of Charles Horsington … . Mrs. Francis asked for leniency on account of her position. She was a widow and big road contractor. She had eight children, three at home, and had been a widow twice. Her act was not done with any intent of stealing and she was very sorry. Mr. Horsington said he had known Mrs. Francis all his life, and he asked the Bench to deal lightly with her, as she had been "pretty well hard put".*

Mrs. Francis said 'If they will keep it out of the papers, I shall very grateful.' Mr Horsington said was never so surprised in all his life when the constable brought Mrs Francis to him. Mrs. Francis (in tears): I was surprised myself. … The woman defendant said '… I asked him not to ruin my character, children and work, and I would be willing to pay anything in reason that I had. P.C. said she added: I am not a thief, it against my religion, and I shall have to go in and confess for this to-morrow'. They were conveyed to Wells, and charged with the offence, when the woman said, "I am very sorry" and Spurle made no reply.

The Chairman said the Bench could not treat a case like this very leniently as it was one of most deliberate theft. They would each be fined £3, and that was treating them leniently. They were each liable to imprisonment." [£3 in 1917 is around £770 in 2018 values].

Who appears on the Roll of Honour?

The next part of this book offers a portrait of the overall experience of each of the men who went to war. Inevitably, we have patchy information about some of these people. Much of the publicly available information comes from official records and from news reports in the Wells Journal. Inevitably, different families received different levels of coverage in the press.

In 1914, the ages of those who went to war ranged between 16 and 44. Their average age, of the 16 men for whom we have reliable information, was around 22. Six were born in Wells and two others for elsewhere in Somerset; three came from London; four from elsewhere in England, and one from Ireland.

In 1914, four of the men were married and living with their wives and their nine children. Frederick Trenchard, the oldest soldier aged 44 in 1914, had five children, two of whom later went to war. They had varied occupations including gardening (4 men), Retail (4 men), paper making (2 men working at the St Cuthbert's Paper Mill in Wookey), and others worked as an organist, scholar, general labourer, an asylum porter and a Railway employee. One was already in the Royal Navy. 6 of the men lived in the 'Southover area' and 8 in the 'city centre', 2 in Wookey, 1 each in Cheddar and Crosscombe.

Four men died in Action. Three are commemorated on the Wells War Memorial at St Cuthbert's churchyard – Joseph Trenchard, Ernest Welsford and Cuthbert Winslow. The fourth soldier who died was William James Read. His name appears on the War memorial at Worle. Two others were receiving a 'war disability pension' in 1939.

The records of the men who served in the Great War are incomplete, largely owing to a major fire during the Second World War and newsprint shortages during the Great War. Consequently, we have only information about the service of 10 of the men. Five served in the Western Front; 2 in Sinai and Palestine; 2 in Mesopotamia and 1 in the Cameroons. All except one were in the army. The other was in the Royal Navy serving on the Cameroons River.

Declaration of war

On 7th August 1914 the Wells Journal reported:

"ENGLAND'S DECLARATION OF WAR The following is the text of the official statement issued by the Government on Tuesday night; "Owing to the summary rejection the German Government of the request made his Majesty's Government that the neutrality of Belgium will be respected; his Majesty's Ambassador in Berlin has received his passport and his Majesty's Government has declared to the German Government that a state of war exists between Great Britain and Germany from 11 p.m. on August 4th.

WHY WE ARE FIGHTING. We are fighting to save a flourishing constitutional kingdom, [Belgium] which has constantly deserved and enjoyed our friendship against a wrong, which no independent State could tolerate without the loss of all its essential liberties (says the Times). We are going into the war, which is forced upon us as the defenders of the weak and the champions the liberties of Europe. If we have to draw the sword, it will be in the same cause for which drew it against Philip 11 and Louis XIV and against Napoleon. It is the cause of right and honour, but it is also the cause of our own vital and immediate interests. The Netherlands and Belgium largely owe their independent existence to the instinct we have ever felt and ever acted on that on no account whatever can England suffer the coasts of the North Sea and the narrow seas over against her own to be at the command of a great military Monarchy, that Monarchy which it may. We cannot rely in such a matter upon undertakings, obligations, or assurances. Would Germany, when she had "dispelled our distrust." respect' them better than she has respected her guarantees to Luxemburg and to Belgium? Her action at this moment the clearest object lesson we could desire of the wisdom of our traditional policy. On that policy, we have even now to act. The necessary steps to make that action prompt and effective has been taken. The King has given the command of the Home Fleet to Sir John Jellicoe, and has appointed Sir John French to be Inspector-General of the Forces are names which will arouse the utmost confidence of his people.

BOOM IN RECRUITING. The mobilisation of the troops has resulted in a great stimulus to recruiting, and the sergeants reaped a harvest on Tuesday, which is without parallel since the time of the Boer War. In the course of the morning scores of youths applied for admission to the Army at the Central Recruiting Office in Great Scotland Yard, and, according to one of the sergeants, they were a promising lot. ... The Naval Recruiting Office also had a busy day. Large crowds gathered outside the various recruiting offices, and the sergeants had a brisk time answering inquiries and giving information to the many who were anxious to know whether or not they were qualified to serve in the King's Army."

THE MEN WHO WENT TO WAR

Nineteen names appeared on the original Roll of Honour in SS Joseph and Teresa's church Wells. Here, the information about each of them is presented in family groups to minimise duplication between entries relating to different members of the same family. The six soldiers for whom we have only limited information appear at the end of this section of the book.

THE FRANCIS – SPURLE FAMILY

William Spurle (b 1898) and Roland Francis (1898) were stepbrothers who served in the First World War and their names appeared on the Roll of Honour.

(Henry) William Spurle (b 1898)

Henry William Spurle was born in Gloucester and was the eldest son of Elizabeth and William Henry Spurle. A younger brother, John known as Jack, arrived in 1900.

His mother, Elizabeth (b 1875) was the youngest daughter of William Spencer, an agricultural labourer living in Wedmore. At the time of the 1891 census, when she was 16 she was working as a Parlour maid at the Wedmore Manor House for John Bailey, a retired solicitor and his family.

She married William Henry Spurle, a boot maker in Gloucester in the first quarter of 1898. He died a couple of months after the 1901 Census and Elizabeth moved back to Somerset with her two young sons.

In spring 1905, she married Arthur Charles Francis of Wookey, a widower since the start of the year. Thus, William Spurle (b 1898) and Roland Francis (1898) became stepbrothers.

Arthur Charles Francis (b 1873)

Arthur Francis Francis was the son of Edward and Hannah Francis from Coxley. Edward was a general haulier and Hannah worked as a laundress. By 1891, Arthur was working at the paper mill in Wookey. Shortly afterwards, he married Ellen Jemima Millard, the daughter of a boot maker from Shepton Mallet.

Ten years later, at the time of the 1901 census, Arthur and Ellen were living in St John's Street, Wells. Arthur was a fishmonger and they had four children Ethel (b 1892), Lena (b 1896), (Arthur) Ronald (b 1898) and Leonard (b 1901). Ellen died in early 1905.

Francis – Spurle Household (from 1905)

Arthur and Elizabeth Francis had at least two children - Alfonso (1907) and Marjorie (1910). At the time of the 1911 census, the family were at Hembury, Wookey. The household included Arthur and Elizabeth together with six children – Ronald (Arthur) and Leonard Francis (from Arthur's first marriage); William and John Spurle (from Elizabeth's first marriage); Alfonso (b 1907) and Marjorie (b 1910). Lena and Ethel are not in the 1911 census return and Ronald was working as a paper sorter at St Cuthbert's Mill, in Wookey.

In April 1912, John Spurle then aged 11, damaged the wall of Mrs Badcock at nearby Somerleaze. He was fined 1s and costs. A little later Ronald Francis may have left home to live in Glastonbury for the Wells Journal reported a misdemeanour in October 1913 saying:

"Arthur Ronald Francis, Hembry Wood, Wookey, was summoned for letting off fireworks in St. Cuthbert-street, on September 27th. —Defendant pleaded guilty. —P.C. Coate stated that at 9.30 p.m. on the date in question he saw defendant let off a squib in St. Cuthbert's Street. He asked him his name, and he replied "Arthur Francis, of Hembry Wood. Wookey", but he found this was not true, because he lived in Redlake, Glastonbury, and had been living there for the last two years. His name was Arthur Ronald, and said his age was in the previous month, whereas they found he was 16 last December. He had given the police a lot of trouble in tracing his address. The letting off a firework in the streets was a frequent occurrence, and the night before the offence, a squib was put through a letterbox and set a mat alight.—Defendant was fined Is. and 6s costs. (Wells Journal - Friday 10 October 1913)

These reports show something of the somewhat chaotic life of the Spurle – Francis household.

Although William Spurle joined the Royal Navy in January 1914, most aspects of life continued relatively unchanged for the Francis – Spurle household. On Whit-Monday in May 1915, the 1st Wells Troop of Boy Scouts under the leadership of Father Morton had enjoyable field day at Ditcheat. The Francis – Spurle family contributed significantly to the success of the day. The Wells Journal reported "… *it was a happy band of 20 scouts, who as soon after the delivery of the morning papers set some of them free, mounted a waggon kindly lent them by Mr. Francis, of Hembry Wood, Wookey. The good mare was driven by one of the scouts. Jack Spurle...*"

Arthur Francis died aged 44 in the autumn of 1915 creating a desperate situation for Elizabeth as seen from in newspaper cutting included at the end of Chapter one.

(Henry) William Spurle at war

It is not clear why Henry William joined the Royal Navy at the start of 1914 but his early upbringing in Gloucester, then a thriving river port, may have been a factor as might the tension between the two families in the household.

Whatever the reason, William was aboard HMS Cumberland when the war started and she went to West Africa. Arriving in August 1914 and they captured 10 German merchant ships in September. HMS Cumberland spent the rest of the war on convoy escort duties and patrolling for German commerce raiders.

In November 1914, the Wells Journal published Henry William's jingoistic and somewhat prejudiced account of the time on the Cameroons River saying:

"ON THE CAMEROON RIVER. Seaman H. W. Spurle, of H.M.S. Cumberland, writing home under date August 24th, to his parents at Wookey, says:—We are up the Cameroon River (German West Africa) bent on capturing the city of Dualo, which is a great German base, and few cruisers up there. We have had several fights with the German forts each side of the river, and captured several ships. One German officer in a small boat had "great inferno machine" fixed on her bows, and was going to blow us up by ramming into us, but in the dark he lost his way, and failed, but saw a gunboat, the Davofv that was with us, and nearly done her in. but it was stopped in the nick of time ... I am full of excitement, and hope we are going into action on Friday against the cussed Germans. We had signal to say they wanted peace, but I hope they will not get it till they are beaten off the face of the earth. We are going to land to-morrow tomorch on Dualo."

In the course of a letter written a little later, he says, *"We have captured Dualo, and are fighting for a brigade a little way up the creek. We are having a pretty good time of it out here, and I hope we shall keep like it. Have had a few casualties, [two killed and a few Marines wounded], but they are getting better. We do not get much news of the Germans here, but I suppose they are getting on all right with their work of slaughtering all Europe, and he (the Kaiser) being Emperor of Europe and King of Africa. I don't think, not while we are in West Africa. He will have to fight for his title."*

In early 1916, the German commander, Carl Zimmermann concluded that the campaign was lost. With Allied forces pressing in on all sides and German resistance faltering, he ordered all remaining German units and civilians to escape to the neutral Spanish colony of Rio Muni. However, the British and French forces remained in the Cameroons until the end of the war.

(Arthur) Ronald Francis at War

Despite his inclusion on the roll of honour, it has not proved possible to trace details of his war service. Ronald married Agnes B K York of Yarley in 1917. She had a greatly troubled childhood in an impoverished family. In 1908, when she was 10, she spent a month in the Wells Workhouse with her sister and six brothers, when her parents went to gaol for neglecting their children and failing to send them to school.

The Spurle / Francis family after the war

We do not know exactly who was living in Elizabeth Francis's household after the end of the war. In 1920, Lena D Francis married George E Vincent, a relative of Joshua Vincent of Wookey who died during the war and listed on the City War Memorial.

John Spurle continued to live with his mother for some time as this press cutting from 1920 illustrates:

"LIGHTING REGULATIONS STILL IN FORCE. Warning to Users of Vehicles. The Chairman of the Wells County Bench of Magistrates (Colonel A. T. Perkins), at a sitting of the Court, on Monday, referred what he feared was a misapprehension in regard to the lighting regulations on the part of users of vehicles on the highway … John Spurle, carter, of Wookey, did not appear to answer a summons for having, on December 4th, at Wookey, driven a horse and cart on the highway, after dark, without the vehicle being provided with proper lights … Fined 10s … [around £50 in 2018 terms]*"* (Wells Journal – 9th January 1920).

In the 1924 Carnival procession, Messrs Spurle and Francis won second prize in the Decorated Motor Cycles and Cycles category for their 'Wookey air mail and ferry' exhibit. On the same occasion, Marjorie Francis, aged 14, appeared as a masquerader called 'Superstitions'.

Relationships between the Spurle and Francis families were not always harmonious as suggested by a news item entitled "Chased with hayfork" (Wells Journal 17 August 1928):

"John Spencer Spurle, [known as Jack], *a seaman of the Sailors' Home, Bristol was summoned for assaulting Alfonso Francis, a farmer of Wookey. Defendant did not appear. Complainant said on the evening of July 20th, they were haymaking. He was collecting and defendant was pitching. After all the hay had been collected, the witness helped to pitch. Spurle asked him to get on the rick, but he told him it was not necessary. Defendant fetched a ladder and went to get on the rick himself. He fell off the ladder, got up and ran after him with a hayfork. Witness ran away home, as he was afraid defendant would do him some harm. When he reached home, he sent for the police. Defendant did not touch him but he would have done so, if he had not ran away.*

Spurle was drunk. Cyrenus Cornish said he was haymaking with Mr. Francis Spurle when he was asked to get on the rick and he told him there was no need of it. W. Spurle then went to the ladder. There was a rung of the ladder missing and the defendant, through being drunk "stepped on the rung which wasn't there." (laughter). Spurle came down and Francis told him it was his own fault. Spurle got up and ran after Francis with the hayfork, and said if he caught him, he would put the fork through him. Francis jumped across a ditch. Spurle tried to get across and fell in.

A letter was read from the defendant, in which he said he was awfully sorry and was unable to attend court because he was sailing that day. He hoped the Bench would take into consideration the drink he had had. He enclosed £1 and said it was all he had, and he hoped the Bench would see their way clear not to fine him anymore. He said that he had now finished with the drink. The Bench imposed a fine of £1 to include the costs of the witnesses."

(Henry) William Spurle's post war life

In 1922, Henry William married Marie E Roberts in Devonport. At the time, he was an able seaman and she purchased his discharge. This marriage seems not to have lasted as he was again at sea in 1924. The records for the ship 'Oononado' show it was engaged in general trade between the USA, West Indies and Avonmouth, sometimes-carrying passengers and the Royal Mail. After a business Henry William and Marie established failed, Marie left him, as he was unable to support her and a child born in 1926. She obtained a divorce in June 1932 when the court heard *'evidence of 'misbehaviour'*.

A year later, he married Rosetta Cunninghame from St. Albans. She died in 1945 at Plymouth. At the time, Henry William was still in the Merchant Navy. He died in 1965 at Southampton and buried in Wookey. The Executrix of his will was Mrs Alice Spurle of 21 Magdalene Street, Glastonbury, Somerset. She was described as his third "wife" although there is no evidence of their marriage.

Ten years after the 'hayfork incident', the following notice appeared in 1938:

"SPURLE John Spencer of 11 Wellington St, Falmouth, Cornwall. d. 24 March 1938 at sea, age 37. Vessel "El Cierve". Administration to Henry William Spurle, Motor Driver and Rosetta Spurle, wife of the said Henry Spurle."

At the time, the El Cierve was sailing from Colon at the Caribbean end of the Panama Canal towards Santos in Brazil.

(Arthur) Roland Francis' life after the war

(Arthur) Roland Francis lived in Wookey after the war continuing in the haulage business run by his father. He appeared in several court cases mainly over minor disputes with neighbours and road accidents. By 1939, he and Agnes were living in a Council House in Wells with two sons – and four other closed entries suggest this was a large family. Closed entries in the 1939 register usually relate to young people who might still be alive today. He was working as a quarryman and his 15-year-old son was a 'cattle food machine operator'. Little is on the public record about his later life. He appears to have been living in Shepton Mallet when he died in 1966 while Agnes died in Wells in 1974.

JAMES HUGH MACMAHON (1896-1979)

James Hugh MacMahon was the son of James and Elizabeth MacMahon of Cheddar. His birth was registered at Axbridge in the autumn of 1896. He had a sister, Kathleen. Their father came from Listowel, Co Kerry, Ireland and married Elizabeth Jane Wide from Taunton. Hugh was a carpenter employed by the Great Western Railway as part of its permanent way staff based in Cheddar.

James was in the army by April 1916 when he attended the funeral of a school friend,

Frederick S. Ridge, at the Baptist Chapel, Cheddar but further details of his military service are missing.

As noted previously James Hugh, often called Hugh, went to the Catholic School in Wells where he met his future wife, Ena Coggan. They both took part in the annual entertainments and both gained scholarships. Their paths separated in 1915 as he joined the army and she moved with her family to Wigan.

We do not know if they remained in contact in this period but the Wells Journal for Friday 12th November 1926 reported:

"Roman Catholic Church of Saints Joseph and Teresa, Wells, was scene on Saturday of a wedding solemnised by the Rev. Father Whittle, between Mr. Hugh James, only son of Mr and Mrs. James McMahon, of Cheddar, and Ena second daughter of Mr. and Mrs. Alfred Coggan of Rowden's road. Wells, The bride, who was given away by her father, was tastefully attired in light blue crepe-de-chine, a bouquet of white carnations. She was attended by one bridesmaid, Miss Nora McMahon, sister of the bridegroom. The newly wed pair left during the afternoon for the honeymoon in London."

James's father was a public-spirited man who as early as 1894 was a member of a group campaigning for street lighting in Cheddar and was involved in Adult education classes. He also held a first aid certificate from his employer. When he died in 1937, the Wells Journal recalled that *'He was chairman of Cheddar Liberal Association. The senior member in the district of the Hearts of Oak Friendly Society, and also a member of the Ancient Order of Druids. He served in the Duke of Cornwall's Light Infantry in pre-war days, and was a past chairman of Cheddar Association Football Club.'* It continued by saying *'Knights of St. Columba, of which Mr. McMahon was a member of the Wells Council, was represented by D. J. McGarvey and Messrs. K. and J. Welsford, P. Mellor, T. Clifford and F. J. Clark.'*

In 1939, James and Ena were living at Worle, near Weston super Mere. He was a Great Western Railway stationmaster and she undertook 'unpaid domestic duties'. It is not clear which station he was responsible for as Worle Parkway Station did not open until 1960. There was an earlier station called Puxton and Worle that closed in 1964. James Hugh died at Weymouth in March 1979 and Ena at Weymouth in 1993.

BERNARD MATHU (1896 – 1953)

David Bernard Mathu (b October 1896) was the son of Dr David Jacob Aaron Chowry Muthu and Mrs Margarita Mathu (née Fox) who married in spring 1891. He was christened on 26th November 1896 at St Mary's Catholic Church, Moorfields. In line with the custom of the time, he was christened using Latin forms of his chosen names i.e. Davidicus Bernardus Muthu. His birth certificate issued in January 1897 at Islington used English names.

Bernard's Catholic faith came from his mother, Margaret Carkeet Fox who was born into a well-known London Catholic family in January 1864. The Fox family had been Catholics for several generations and were eminent physicians. Her grandfather, Charles James Fox (1799 – 1874), studied medicine in Edinburgh and at London's Consumption Hospital before becoming a consulting-physician to the Spanish and Portuguese Jews' Hospital and the Royal Hospital for Diseases of the Chest. After the Roman Catholic Relief Act 1829, he became physician to the leading members of the emerging Catholic hierarchy. Margaret's father, Charles James Fox (1829-1895), M.D., M.R.C.S., L.R.C.P., was also a leading physician in his generation.

Bernard's father was born in 1865 near Madras, now known as Chennai. Chowry's father worked as a preventative officer with the Indian Customs service. Chowry had five siblings including Rev. Samuel Aaron, Joshua Abraham, Isaac Jacob and a sister. The prevalence of biblical names indicates that the family were probably Christians. The district had a long association with Christianity derived from the the tradition that Thomas the Apostle went to India to preach the Gospel and reached Tamil Nadu and Kerala in about 50 AD. Historically, this Christian community was organised as the Province of India of the Church of the East, served by Nestorian bishops and a local dynastic Archdeacon. The Church of the East declined after the 16th century due to outside influences including the Islamic invasion and the arrival of Portuguese missionaries. Might the Chowry family's Christian faith have been sustained through these events?

Chowry was one of a small group of Indian men who came to Britain in the final quarter of the nineteenth century. He studied medicine in the 1880s; graduating from King's College, London as a physician and surgeon. He moved into general practice and began to specialise in treating tuberculosis. At this stage in his life, he started to become an indefatigable campaigner on a range of social, political and medical issues. These included novel medical treatments, lifestyle improvements, vegetarianism, nutrition, temperance, poverty, human and political rights in India, and Yogic Philosophy. Many of his themes drew on traditional Indian teaching, values and beliefs.

Chowry was not a Catholic but once in Britain, he took part in many Christian events and wrote at least one hymn. In 1892, he founded the Indian Christian Society of Great Britain with the aim of helping his co-religionists from India settle in England.

In June 1887, the Kent & Sussex Courier reported *"CHURCH OF ENGLAND ZENANA MISSIONARY SOCIETY ... TUNBRIDGE WELLS ASSOCIATION. The Annual Meeting will be held on Tuesday, June 7th at 8 o'clock, at the Great Hall. ... when information regarding the needs of the women of India and the work of the Society will be given by W. B. Harington, Esq., Public Works Dept., (India) and Chowry Muthu, A Native Christian Gentleman."* An Anglican Zenana missions developed sought to break down the barriers to women receiving medical care in countries where the segregation of men and women preventing easy access to medical care mostly provided by male doctors.

At the time of the 1891 census, he was single, living in Ilford, Essex and working as a general practitioner. A few weeks later, he married Margaret Carkeet Fox in Hendon. They may have met through her father's position as a leading authority on the treatment of tuberculosis. In time, they had five children: Dorothy (1892 – Romford), Olive (1895 – Islington), Bernard (1897 – Islington), Philip Leslie (1901 – Isle of Wight) and Cecilia Mary (1902 Isle of Wight).

In 1892, he became the superintendent of the Inglewood Sanatorium at Ventnor on the Isle of Wight linking his growing professional reputation to that of the Sanatorium. The Dundee Evening Telegraph for Wednesday 19 March 1902 reported, *"One of the finest is the Inglewood Sanatorium, presided over by Dr Chowry Muthu, one of our recognised authorities on phthisis, and pioneer of the open-air treatment. He holds—and with reason— that if taken in time the disease is almost always curable. The old-fashioned idea that once a person has contracted tuberculosis he is doomed man is, thanks to indefatigable workers like Dr Muthu, entirely exploded."* (Phthisis is another term for pulmonary tuberculosis or similar progressive wasting diseases.)

After the turn of the century, he began to attend the annual meetings of the British Medical Association (BMA). By 1905, he was presenting papers to its meetings and those of the Royal Society of Medicine and of the Psychotherapeutic Society.

The Muthu family life in Wells

By September 1904, the Muthu family were in Wells as the Shepton Mallet Journal reported *'The Wesley Guild, on the invitation of Dr and Mrs. Muthu, paid a visit to the Sanatorium at Hillgrove, the visit being much enjoyed'*. He remained the superintendent of Hillgrove for over twenty years. Hillgrove Sanatorium at Green Ore was one of five sanatoria in Somerset.

During this time, the family lived at Hillgrove and on Portway, close to Wells city centre. The household included a governess to look after and educate the younger children. David spent much of time on numerous speaking engagements, writing and visits to India alongside his duties in Wells.

The family settled into a comfortable middle class life in Wells with the children attending good schools and undertaking a range of artistic and sporting endeavours. Dorothy showed an early interest in music, playing in public concerts at St Thomas's church and Hillgrove. Olive won prizes for drawing and for her costumes at fancy dress balls; and both helped at the 1913 Jumble Sale in aid of the Nursing Association and with later by raising money for Belgian refugees, the Red Cross Hospital and general war related funds led by the Mayor.

The 1911 census shows David and four of his children at Hillgrove and Dorothy as staying with the children of the Bowning family at Wick House, Coxley. Robert

Bowning was the mayor of Wells in 1904. Margaret did not appear in the 1911 Census. Bernard went to the 'Cathedral Grammar School', a forerunner of the Cathedral School, where he seems to take a greater interest in sport than his academic studies. He passed his Preliminary Oxford Local Examinations as an 'over age' candidate in 1912 but did not progress to higher-level examinations in later years. On the sports field he was well placed in several events in 1911 including the 100 yards, quarter-mile and high jump; and in 1912 the 100 yards and three-legged races. An unspecified Muthu (probably Olive aged 14) won a prize for general progress at the Wells Grammar School in 1909. David's interest in 'outdoor treatments used at the Inglewood and Hillgrove Sanatoriums may have drawn on his interest in the work of Ebenezer Howard who inspired the 'Garden City Movement' that achieved early successes in Letchworth, Welwyn and Hampstead. In 1910, David Muthu wrote *'it has been shown by the open-air, the garden city, and other movements, that fresh air and sunlight, beautiful and healthy surroundings, are essential for the sound development of body and mind, and for the growth of child-life… If men and women are to grow physically and morally strong, and derive pleasure and inspiration from their environment, they must have healthy homes and aesthetic surroundings'.*

By the time of the 1918 General Election, it became clear that there was an acute shortage of housing that many returning soldiers could afford. A new social attitude focused the Government's attention on a national responsibility to provide homes, giving rise to Lloyd George's famous promise of 'homes fit for heroes'. The new housing schemes, including those in Wells occupied by some of the Catholic soldiers, reflected the ideas of the 'garden city' movement including those of David.

David published several books, two of which are still in print. He wrote the first while he was in Wells. It is *'Pulmonary tuberculosis: its etiology and treatment, a record of 10 years' observation and work in open-air sanatoria'* (1910 updated 1922). (Etiology is the cause, set of causes, or manner of causation of a disease or condition) The second is 'The antiquity of Hindu Medicine' (1931).

Bernard goes to war

The Wells Journal's Roll of Honour includes Bernard's service as being with the 2/16th Battalion of the County of London Queen's Westminster Rifles. The first entry showing him on the front line was on 11th August 1916. He remained 'In the fighting line' until at least 2nd March 1917 (when the Wells Journal ceased publishing the full Roll of Honour) due to paper shortages.

The 2/16th served as part of 179th (2/4th London) Brigade. It is not possible to identify exactly where Bernard served from the published records. During his time 'on the fighting line', the Brigade served in France (June – December 1916), Salonika (December 1916 – June 1917), Palestine (June 1917 – March 1918) and France (April 1918 – November 1918). Whilst in the Middle East, the 2/4th London Brigade was part of the force led by the Indian Army.

Just after Bernard went into the 'fighting line', the Wells Journal (Friday 13 October 1916) reported:

"The engagement is announced between Dorothy Mary Carkeet, elder daughter of C. Muthu, M.D., M.R.C.S., L.R.C.P., and Mrs. Muthu, of Mendip Hills Sanatorium, and Portway. Wells, and grand-daughter of the late Charles James Fox, M.D., M.R.C.S., L.R.C.P.: and Saral Kumar Ray, barrister of the High Court of Calcutta, son of P. K. Ray, D.Sc. Lond and Edin.), of the Indian Educational Service, and Mrs. Sarala Ray, and grandson of the late Mr. D. M. Das, eminent social reformer of Calcutta, India".

From this, it is clear that the Muthu family was developing strong links with the leading families in post-war India. It is not clear when or where the wedding took place. However, Dorothy was an unaccompanied passenger using her married name on the P&O ship 'Sicilia' sailing for Bombay in November 1921.

After the war, David spent an increasing part of his time in India while continuing as the superintendent at Hillgrove. One of the friends he made in these years was Mahatma Gandhi, who shared his views on natural cures and other aspects of living a 'good life'. When in the UK, Dr Muthu was a ready reference for British newspapers on India and in particular Gandhi. Press reports demonstrate that he continued to be a frequent public speaker on many subjects.

Bernard was back in Wells by 1920 when the Wells Journal (5th March 1920) reported *"Bernard Muthu, a student at the Grove Hill Sanatorium, near Wells, pleaded guilty to riding a bicycle without a rear light on the Glastonbury Road, 9.45 p.m. on the 22nd February, and was fined 7/6."* (Around £100 in 2018 prices.)

This was a short visit as in the autumn of 1920 he started a course in London for a preliminary examination in arts completed in 1922. He went on to undertake preparatory medical study at the newly opened Chelsea Polytechnic, although he seems not to have completed this course. For a time he lived with his parents in Belsize Avenue, London NW 3.

His married sister, Dorothy, was in Wells in 1923 when the Wells Journal (28 September 1923) reported: *"ENTERTAINMENT. On Saturday evening last, the students of the Wells Theological College gave a concert for the patients of the Mendip Hills Sanatorium. Mrs. Dorothy Ray presided at the piano. Besides songs, duets, etc., two short plays "Sherlock Homes" and "A Pair of Spectacles" were performed, in which the 'Rev. and Mrs. Fyffe and Mr. O'Reilly took part. After a very enjoyable evening was brought to a close by Dr Muthu who proposed a very cordial vote of thanks to the visitors."*

On 25 September 1925, the Wells Journal published three items of Muthu family news: *"BIRTH – RAY on the 15th ult. Simla, the Hon. K. C. and Mrs. Dorothy Ray, (nee Muthu), a daughter (Indira Margarita)*

MARRIAGES - MUTHU - BELL. — On the 16th inst. at the Brompton Oratory … Leslie Philip, youngest son of Dr and Mrs. Muthu, of Belsize Avenue, Hampstead, and late of Hillgrove, Wells, Somerset, to Miriam Philomena, fourth daughter of Mr. and Mrs. Sydney Joseph Bell, of Park Farm, South Stoke, Grantham.

DEATHS – FOX On the 14th ult., at Wrotham Heath, Kent, fortified by the rites of Holy Church, Francis John Fox, R.N.R., late P. and 0., second son of the late Charles James Fox, M.R.C.S., L.R.C.P., London, and brother Mrs. Chowry Muthu."

Two months later, details of Olive Muthu's wedding appeared in the Wells Journal (Friday 27 November 1925):

"FASHIONABLE WEDDING IN LONDON. MISS OLIVE MUTHU AND MR. J. K DASGUPTA.
A ceremony which will be of interest to her many friends in Wells, took place on Saturday afternoon, the 14th inst., at the Brompton Oratory, South Kensington, when Olive Cecilia, younger daughter of C. Muthu, M.D., L.R.C.P., etc., and Mrs. Muthu, of Belsize Avenue, Hampstead, late of Hillgrove, Wells, Somerset, and grand-daughter of the late Charles James Fox, M.R.C.P., L.R.C.P., was married to Mr. J. K. Dasgupta, Barrister at Law, and nephew of the Hon. S. E. Das, Executive Member of the Viceroy's Council, India.

The bride, who was given away by her brother, Mr. Bernard D. Muthu, looked beautiful in a long ivory satin gown trimmed with fur, designed and made by Madame Marguerite Owers, Court Dressmakers, of Haringay. … She also carried a bouquet of white carnations, roses and lilies of the valley, and was attended by Miss Cecilia Reid, as bridesmaid. P. Dansie, of Coventry acted as best man, and carried out his duties most admirably.

The ceremony was performed by the Rev. Father McNabb, O.P., of the Dominican Priory, Hampstead, during which the organ played soft music, but as the wedding couple left the altar and proceeded down the aisle to their car, it pealed forth the Wedding March. The reception was held at Belsize Avenue at which some fifty guests were present. The wedding presents which numerous and valuable, included many cheques. The honeymoon was spent at Frinton-on-Sea."

Olive's choice of husband shows that she, like her sister, was moving into the the leading ranks of pre-independence Indian Society. The Viceroy's Executive Council was the cabinet of the government of British India but it is not clear what role S E Das performed.

Although the family left Wells in about 1924, David remained superintendent at Hillgrove until 1927.

The Wells Journal announced the closure of Hillgrove on 1st April 1927 saying: *"HILL GROVE SANATORIUM. We learn with regret to-day that the Hillgrove Sanatorium for the cure of consumption is to permanently close down. Dr Chowry Muthu the eminent authority Tuberculosis is returning to India in the near future. Thus will Wells lose another institution which has considerably assisted its trade."*

Later on 3rd August 1928, the Journal reported *"DEATH. —On Tuesday, July 11th, 1928 at 48, Avenue, Hampstead, NW3. Margaret Carkeet (nee Fox), wife Dr Muthu, late Hill Grove, Somerset. Fortified by the rites of the Holy Church. A loyal wife, devoted mother, a loving sister and faithful friend."*

In 1928, Bernard married Celia M Reid, his sister's bridesmaid, in Holborn. In 1939, she was living in Hendon with her mother and brother, and her status was given as 'single'. She worked as a bank clerk. David Bernard was not included in the 1939 register.

Muthu family's post war life in India

Shortly after the end of the Great War, Chowry hit upon the idea of opening a sanatorium for people with tuberculosis in India. Before opening his sanatorium, he made an extensive study of existing facilities across the country. In 1923, he attended the Tuberculosis Conference in Lucknow and then submitted a memorandum to the Madras Government on the necessity of establishing a sanatorium in the area. They accepted his proposal and he opened a sanatorium at Tambaram.

In 1939, Dr Muthu married for a second time to Ena W Cox from Hornsey, North London. He was 66 and she was 34. Evidently, they went to India shortly after the wedding where David died on 7th May 1940. He is buried at the St Andrews (Church of Scotland) in Bangalore, about 200 miles from his birthplace.

In 1933, Bernard was working in the Accounts Department of the India Office. In 1939, he was a clerical officer in the Stores Department of the India Office, in London. However, he visited India regularly in the 1940s and early 1950s, often staying with cousins at Puraswalkam, a residential and retail area, close to the centre of Chennai. One of his cousins recalls, *'conversing with him was great fun, as he knew no Tamil and she and her siblings very little English. Dining with him was even more entertaining as he used a knife and fork'.* The family recalled that he spent part of his working life in retail banking.

Bernard died at Hendon in the autumn of 1953, aged 56 and buried in Kensal Green Cemetery. Celia died in Hendon in 1984.

THE TRENCHARD FAMILY

The four members of the Trenchard family from Wells served in the army during the Great War. Their family played an important role in the Catholic Community in Wells around the turn of the twentieth century. All four were descended from John Trenchard, born 1829. Three were Trenchards and the fourth was Frederick Clark.

John Trenchard (born 1829) was a fellmonger (or dealer in animal hides) in his youth. He had two wives, in succession, and ten children born between 1853 and 1873. John and Mary, his second wife, had five children (Sarah, Benjamin, John Jnr, Frederick and Lucy). Frederick Trenchard and two of his sons lived in Wells and fought in the Great War – as did Frederick Clark, his nephew. Doubtless, other members of John's extended family also served in the forces - some of whom would have been almost unknown to Frederick and his family.

In 1871, the Trenchards were in Taunton living with six children. By 1873, when the final child, Lucy was born, the family lived in Glastonbury where John worked as a gardener, as did Frederick the eldest son.

Ten years later, they were living at 22 Union Street, Wells with the four youngest children and two boarders. One daughter Francis Elizabeth was in Cardiff working as a general domestic servant for William Jones, a ship's pilot, his wife and five sons. Another daughter, Mary Rose who married in 1878, was in Kentish Town with her husband, William John Clark and two children. Her Husband came originally from Bath and worked as a builder's manager.

In January 1882, John Trenchard was looking for *"A Piece of GARDEN or ALLOTMENT GROUND, quarter of acre or less, in or near Wells. Send particulars to JOHN TRENCHARD. 22, Union Street, Wells."* (Wells Journal - Thursday 26 January 1882).

By 1891, John and Mary Trenchard's family were living at Mount Pleasant, Wookey Hole Lane with two sons, and an adult daughter (Ellen) and a granddaughter (Rose Clark born in London). John Snr and Frederick were gardeners; Benjamin was a farmer and Mary a laundress. In the same year, (Frances) Elizabeth Trenchard (b 1861) was one of two servants looking after Father John Berard, the 'chaplain at the Convent' in Chamberlain Street.

In December 1892, Benjamin appeared in the police Court, summoned by William Embry, a grocer, of High street, Wells, charged with assaulting him on 25th October. This related to a dispute that arose some months earlier when Mr Embry employed Benjamin's sister, Lucy Trenchard as a household servant. Following an exchange of insults, Benjamin hit William Embry. Benjamin's solicitor argued that the incident had been provoked by intemperate language on the part of Mr Embry. The Bench considered there was some justification for the assault, and fined the defendant 1s., and costs 11s. 6d (about £22 and £250 in 2018 values respectively).

The following decade saw important changes in the Trenchard family life. In 1893, the home in Wookey Hole Road was the subject of a compulsory purchase order for a road-widening scheme. Two years later John Snr. was selling hay, straw, apples and farm equipment as he was *'giving up the farm'*. The family appear to have moved to Bathes House on Ash Lane.

In 1895, Frederick Trenchard married Sarah Jane King in Tynemouth. It is unclear why the marriage took place there. Sarah was born at Peshawar India in 1863 close to the volatile Afghan border. She was the daughter of James and Susannah King. Indian records suggest that her father died shortly after she was born. As she does not appear in the 1881 Census for Great Britain, she and her mother may have remained in India until she was grown up. In 1891, she was a boarder at St Mary's Convent in Chamberlain Street.

On 14th June of 1897, John Trenchard Snr died at the age of 67. Just before his death, he contributed 6d (about £10) to the Queen Victoria's Diamond Jubilee fund for 'General Rejoicings'. At around this time Frederick and Sarah returned to Wells with their newborn son, Joseph John.

In 1901, there were at least three Trenchard households in or near Wells:

- John's widow, Mary had moved from Wookey Hole Road to The Bathes, Wells, and was living with her unmarried son, Benjamin; Ellen and Josephine (daughters) both laundresses; and a granddaughter, Susannah Trenchard (b 1896). Mary died in 1904.

- Fredrick Trenchard lived at 17 Rowdens Road, Wells with Sarah, his wife; two sons, Joseph and James; and May, his daughter – and three lodgers. He was a gardener. Sometime later, he moved to 5 Priory Place, St John Street. One of the lodgers, James King a stonecutter, may have been Sarah's relative.

- Frederick's unmarried sister, Frances E Trenchard (born 1861) was housekeeper to Father Carroll at St Michael's church at East Harptree. In 1937, the Wells Journal reported her death saying:

"DEATH OF MISS TRENCHARD The death occurred suddenly on Christmas Day from a heart attack at the residence of her nephew [James], 29, Barley Close, of Miss Frances Elizabeth Trenchard. Miss Trenchard was housekeeper to the Rev. Father Carroll, for 30 years at Bristol, East Harptree and Shepton Mallet. She was 76 years of age. The funeral took place on Tuesday morning. A service was held at the Catholic Church of SS. Joseph and Teresa, conducted by the Rev. Father McHenry, assisted by the Rev. Father Metcalfe. The burial followed at Wells Cemetery. The mourners were; Messrs. F. A. Clark, J. J Trenchard and B. Clark, nephews; Misses W. Clark, M. Clark, B. Clark, C. Clark, nieces; Mr. P. Clark, Mr. A. Clark, Nephews, Mrs J Trenchard, niece. "(Wells Journal - Friday 31 December 1937)

In 1905, an advertisement referred to Frederick's household:

"7 LONG-LEASEHOLD DWELLING-HOUSES and Premises, known as 1, 2, 3, 4, 5, 6, and 7, Priory place, St. John-street, Wells, together with the Gardens in front thereof,

in respective occupation of:— 1, Mr. Bloodworth ; 2, Mr. Gibbons ; 3, Mr. Hawkins: 4, Mr, Smart; 5, Mr. Trenchard; 6. Mrs. Bedford ; 7, Mr. Brown The whole of the Premises are held under a Lease dated in 1859 for the term of 150 years, at the annual rent of £3 …The gross rents amount to £9 13s 0d, The Corporation Water is laid on to each house, and the sanitary arrangements have recently been put in excellent order. For further particulars, apply to the 25, Market-place, Wells, or to SIDNEY F. GOODALL, Solicitor, Wells." The gross rents were equivalent to around £1,200 in 2018 prices.

In the same year, Frederick Trenchard appeared in the electoral register for Priory Place while Benjamin was at Milton Lane. In 1907, Benjamin was petitioning the City Council to make improvements to the services provided on Milton Lane, especially street lighting and sewers.

On 24th October 1908, Benjamin died at 7, Jubilee Terrace, Portway, Wells. He married shortly before his death and this explains this advertisement:

"HOUSEHOLD EFFECTS FOR SALE BY PRIVATE TREATY. MRS. TRENCHARD, Portway, Wells, has decided to dispose of all her HOUSEHOLD EFFECTS, including a quantity of New Household Linen, Contents of Sitting room and Parlour, Kitchen and Bedrooms. On view at the above address, from Thursday, Nov. 19th to Wednesday, Nov. 26th. No reasonable offer refused." (Wells Journal - Thursday 19 November 1908)

Around this time, younger members of the Trenchard family were playing important roles in the 'annual entertainments' provided by the children at the Catholic school. James and Dolly Trenchard appeared in the 1907 and 1908 shows. Dolly was probably Mary Freda Anthony Trenchard (b 1898). Others in the cast include members of the McMahon and Welsford families whose names appear alongside James's on the Roll of Honour.

In 1911, there were two Trenchard households in Wells. Frederick was in Priory Place with Sarah, two sons (James and Joseph) and three daughters (Mary, Sarah and Helena). Meanwhile, Ellen had moved to 24 Chamberlain Street and was living with her three sisters (Laura, Josephine and Lucy); Suzanne, her niece; and three members of the Clark family from Kentish Town – Frederick Clark (aged 20 and a groundsman) and his sisters Gertrude and Phyllis (both at school).

In May 1924, Ellen Trenchard, by then almost 70 was still running her boarding house opposite the Catholic Church. We know this because the Wells Journal reported that *'Ellen Trenchard, of Chamberlain Street, was summoned for the non-payment of the Poor Rate costs of £4 /7 /-, (around £235 in 2018 prices) and the non-payment of the District Rate and costs, £3/10/- (around £190 in 2018 prices). Defendant said she had one lodger, who was leaving on Saturday. She could not pay the demand. Mr. Wilcox said it was the auditor who directed that the defendant must be summoned. The Bench decided on the case of the Poor*

Rate to adjourn the summons for month, and refer the matter to the overseers" Ellen died in January 1925.

Towards the end of 1912, Suzanne Trenchard married her cousin, Frederick Clark. Their first child, Benjamin was born in the third quarter of 1914; at just about the time Frederick left for war. During the war, they had a further son and daughter and subsequently six further children.

Just before the outbreak of war, three members of the Trenchard family worked as gardeners – Frederick and James Trenchard, and Frederick Clark. It is not clear, whether they operated together as a small business or if they operated independently. Frederick looked after the convent garden in Chamberlain Street at this time.

Two members of the family were amongst the first to enlist leaving the city on 1ˢᵗ September 1914 – 27 days after the outbreak of the war.

RECRUITS FROM WELLS Several batches of recruits have left Wells during the week for Taunton. ... Tuesday witnessed the departure of other Wells men. These including ... F. A. Clark, J. Trenchard (St. John street) ... There was a large number about in the Market Place to see these men depart, and the Mayor and Town Clerk (Mr. E. P. Foster) again accompanied the recruits to the station, where there were enthusiastic scenes. (Wells Journal - Friday 4 September 1914)

James Trenchard at war

James joined the army at Shepton Mallet on 31 August 1914 following general call for volunteers to serve overseas or in the empire. He became a gunner with the Somerset Royal Horse Artillery (RHA) that had light, mobile, horse-drawn guns. The recruits went to Wivenhoe (Essex) on 4th September 1914 as part of a Reserve Unit.

On 14th February 1916, they transferred to the First Line and sailed from Devonport for Alexandria in Egypt. In March, four British Territorial RHA batteries were assigned to provide artillery support for the ANZAC (Australia and New Zealand Army Corps) Mounted Division. They served with the Desert Column in the Sinai and Palestine Campaign from the Battle of Magdhaba (23 December 1916) until the Second Battle of Gaza (17 – 19 April 1917).

In July 1917, the Somerset RHA was attached to to the 1ˢᵗ Light Horse Brigade. As part of the Desert Mounted Corps, they took part in the capture of Beersheba (31 October), the Battle of Mughar Ridge (13 and 14 November) and the defence of Jerusalem against the Turkish counter-attacks (27 November – 3 December).

At the beginning of 1918, the division was attached to XX Corps and helped to capture Jericho (19 –21 February) and then took part in the First Trans-Jordan Raid (21 March

– 2 April). It returned to the Desert Mounted Corps for the Second Trans-Jordan Raid (30 April – 4 May), the Battle of Abu Tellul (14 July) and the capture of Amman (25 September). This was about a month before the Ottoman Empire agreed to the Armistice of Mudros on 30 October 1918, ending the Sinai and Palestine Campaigns.

In early September 1918, James wrote to his mother from Jerusalem and an extract appeared in the Wells Journal:

"A Letter from 'Palestine. — The following an extract from a letter received by Mrs. F. Trenchard, of Priory-place, from her son, Gunner J. Trenchard, serving in Palestine: —

You will be pleased to have some news about the Catholic soldiers in Palestine. First, we had procession to the Holy City of Jerusalem, on the Feast of Our Lady's Assumption. [15th August] There we had Holy Mass, and over 2,000 Catholic soldiers went Confession and Holy Communion. Then we all had breakfast, and afterwards marched to Jaffa, where we said the Joyful Mysteries of the Rosary. Later we marched to the Church the Holy Sepulchre, where we sang hymns and said the Sorrowful Mysteries. We then proceeded to the Tomb of Our Lady, where completed the Rosary and said the Profundis for all the soldiers fallen in the war, and finished at the Church of St Stephen with the Stations of The Cross and the Benediction Service. It was a grand sight, the first time it has been seen for many years. (Wells Journal - Friday 27 September 1918*)*

James's life after the war

After the war, James went to work at the Underwood Quarry run by the Somerset County Council where his father also worked. He was active in arranging social events and outings for other employees. By 1929, he was a steam lorry driver's mate.

Towards the end of 1924, James married Winifred Redman, from Chard, who died early in 1925. This may have been in childbirth as a daughter; also called Winifred arrived in the first quarter of 1925. In the following year, he married Frances Sarah Hedges, the daughter of Charles Hedges, a gamekeeper employed by Mr. C. C. Tudway of Milton Lodge. They had two children - Joseph born in 1928 and Susan in 1946. Sadly, Susan seems to have died in the same quarter as she was born.

James was active in many areas of social life and featured in many articles in the Wells Journal. These events included organising and participating in Whist Drives; acting as the Master of Ceremonies at social events for the Catholic Church; organising sporting events; growing and showing prize vegetables; acting as the chief marshal and later as a committee member for the Wells Carnival; being a member of the local Labour Party's management committee; and playing Santa Claus at the Catholic Church's Christmas bazaar. He also represented the group of former Royal Artillery soldiers in the city at many memorial ceremonies and funerals.

Apart from these positive reports of his activities, he had one minor brush with the law in 1950. *"Nine local wireless owners failed to take our advice and result they appeared at Wells City Petty Sessions on Tuesday and had to plead guilty to working a wireless set without a licence. …. The first defendant was James I. A. Trenchard, of 18, Barley Close, and Mr. Douglas John Chalmers, of Exeter, a Post Office engineer, said that he called at 18, Barley Close and brought the wireless receiver into use. Defendant admitted he had worked the wireless since Christmas, 1949, when it was installed, and said he could not afford the licence. Defendant wrote apologising and pleading guilty."* (Wells Journal, Friday 14 April 1950).

James died in Wells in 1967 and Frances in 1988 at Bristol.

Frederick Clark at War

In 1911, Frederic Clark and two of his sisters were living in Wells as part of Ellen Trenchard's household and working as a groundsman, possibly with his uncle and cousin. Later, he worked at St Cuthbert's Paper Mill and his name appears in the membership records of the National Union of Printing & Paper Workers as all paper workers in the forces appeared automatically in the union's records. His cousin, Joseph Trenchard, also worked at the St Cuthbert's Mill, Wookey and his name is on the Company's War memorial in its reception area.

Frederick Clark enlisted for war service in September 1914. His attestation papers - the record of the information he gave to the recruiting officer showed his occupations as gravedigger and gardener. He joined the 705th Labour Company, 6th Battalion of the Royal Engineers. As such, he was part of the units formed of 'men of the navvy class' and those who were over military age or not fit for front line combat service because of wounds, injury or illness. They undertook the the immense task of building and maintaining the huge network of roads, railways, canals, buildings, camps, trenches, stores, dumps, telegraph and telephone systems needed to bring men, materials and communications to the frontline. By 1917, Frederick was one of the 389,900 men (more than 10% of the British Army) working on such tasks – half of them overseas, often within range of the enemy guns, sometimes for lengthy periods. In June 1915, both the Royal Engineer and infantry labour battalions went overseas for work in army areas, mainly on road maintenance. Later, these units became part of Labour Corps providing much of the effort needed to clear the battlefields across Europe following the 1918 armistice. We do not know if Frederick served in Britain or overseas

Frederick Clark's life after the war

When Frederick arrived back in Wells, he was the head of a household with three children with a further six to arrive over the following decade. Unlike other members of the family, he attracted little attention in the local press so it is difficult to be certain about many aspects of his life. He seems to have appealed unsuccessfully against a decision not to award a war pension on the grounds of damage to his eyesight. He may have been the Mr F Clark who with others represented the General Post Office at Kenrick Welsford's funeral in 1946.

Frederick and Suzanne had six further children, the final being Constance in 1930. Suzanne died in the late summer of 1931:

"MRS. S CLARKE The death occurred on Monday morning at residence, 1, Church Avenue, Wells, Mrs. Clarke, wife Mr. F. A. Clarke. Deceased was only 35 years of age. The greatest sympathy is extended to Mr. Clarke and his young children in their great loss. The funeral took place at Wells Cemetery this Thursday morning, the Rev. Father Whittle officiating." (Wells Journal - Friday 10 July 1931).

In 1925, Frederick's son, Benjamin received a scholarship to attend the Blue School and in 1930 won the school's history prize. During the 1930s, Benjamin was active in local politics writing numerous letters to the Wells Journal on a diverse range of subjects. His younger sister shared this interest in politics and both were active in the Labour Party after the Second World War.

During the 1930s, Frederick's daughters followed in the family tradition of performing in the 'annual entertainments' provided by the Catholic School. In 1935, Frederick's eldest daughter, Winifred married Frederick W Wright of Clutton.

The 1939 Register throws some light on Frederick's household at Hervey Road where they lived. Frederick was 49 years old and worked as a cheese warehouseman. His daughter, Phyllis (16) was a cheese packer. Others in the household were Benjamin (24) was a factory clerk, Marie (18) a checker for a boot and slipper manufacturer, and Constance (9) was at school. His son, Frederick J A Clark, a former Railway clerk was "incapacitated by TB" and Rose Clark, Frederick's mother aged 85 was living with the family "Incapacitated by age". Frederick, his son, died in 1941 and Rose in 1942. There were four other members of the household but the National Archives have yet to release the details. Frederick died in Bath in 1980.

Frederick Trenchard at war

Frederick Trenchard joined the army in 1915 becoming a pioneer in the Royal Engineers. He was at the front during 1915 and transferred to the newly formed 9th Labour Battalion as part of the 5th Army in October 1916. The 5th army participated in the Battle of the Ancre - the final British effort in the Battle of the Somme, the Battle of Arras and the Third Battle of Ypres. In March 1918, the 5th Army took over a stretch of front-line south of the River Somme that bore the brunt of the opening phase of the German Spring Offensive. The failure of the Fifth Army to withstand the German advance led to its disbandment. Although reformed, it saw little action in the remainder of the war. It is not clear when Frederick was demobilised and returned to Wells.

Frederick's life after the war

In the 1920s, Frederick started work as a handyman and cleaner at the County Council operated Underwood Quarry. Three years later, he was one of the nine-man organising committee for the highly successful workforce's summer outing to Weymouth.

In June 1923, the Wells Journal reported:

"MOTOR CYCLES COLLIDE. A somewhat alarming collision took place in Portway about 8 o'clock on Sunday evening, when two motor cycles, one with a sidecar, came into violent contact. The driver of one of the cycles was Mr. B. Dyer, of Brent Knoll, near Burnham, who had his wife with him in the sidecar. The other cycle was driven by Mr. A. E. Batstone of Wells, and he had with him Miss Sarah Trenchard, [Frederick's daughter] also of Wells, and she was riding on the pillion. Mr. Dyer was on his way home and Mr. Batstone was riding into Wells, and as the cyclists were approaching the turning into Chamberlain Street they saw each other, but too late to avoid each other, with the result that they came into violent collision. The riders and their passengers were thrown out, Miss Trenchard was severely shaken up and was taken into a house close by. Mrs. Dyer was unhurt, but Mr. Dyer's hands were cut about. Mr. Batstone escaped injury, but the front wheel of his machine was so buckled that he was unable to ride it home, front lamp was also broken Mr. Dyer's machine was also slightly damaged, but he was able to proceed on his journey." (Wells Journal - Friday 15 June 1923)

This accident does not seem to have affected unduly the relationship between Sarah and Arthur Batstone as they married early in 1926. Later that year, Frederick and Arthur won the award for the most original item in the Carnival procession with their entry "A Toast to the Carnival", consisting of a representation of a huge bottle of old port and a decorated loving cup. Sarah's sister, Helena (known as Nellie) won an award as an Individual 'Masquerade' called 'Irish Colleen'.

Frederick Trenchard died on 3rd May 1932 following an accident at the Underwood Quarry. A reversing steam lorry knocked Frederick down and both his legs were run over. He died almost immediately at the scene. At the time, Sarah his wife, was his only dependant and she received £300 compensation awarded by the inquest - £25 immediately and the rest at £2 a month - equivalent to around £50,000 in 2018 terms. This was one of many accidents at the quarry reported in the Wells Journal in the previous decade. In the 1930s, Kenrick Welsford, a well-known City Councillor, an ex-serviceman and fellow Catholic represented the quarry workers in many disputes over safety at the quarry.

Frederick's funeral took place in the same week as the inquest. The Wells Journal reported:

"THE FUNERAL. LARGE GATHERING AT CEMETERY. The funeral took place at Wells Cemetery on Sunday afternoon and the esteem in which deceased was held was evidenced by the large number attending the service.

About thirty of his workmates at Underwood Quarry with Mr. G. F. Norris (manager), and Mr. T. Gadd (foreman), preceded the coffin; also a number of ex-servicemen, including Capt. J. C. Toomer, Messrs. R. Packer, C. Marsh and K. Welsford; members of the Wells lodge of Buffaloes, and members of the Rose and Crown Thrift Club, of which deceased was a member of the Committee. The coffin was covered with a Union Jack, deceased having served with the Labour Battalion during the Great War. The service was conducted by the Rev. Father Whittle. The mourners were Jim (son), Sally and Nellie (daughters), sister Laura, Messrs. H. Loxton (son-in law), G. Brown (nephew), F. Clark (nephew), Winnie Clark (niece) Bennie and Fred Clark (nephews), Mr. W. Stevens (friend).

On arriving at the Cemetery, the brethren of the Wookey Hole Lodge of Buffaloes lined the pathway. After the coffin had been lowered into the grave, the brethren of the RAOB filed past dropping their sprigs of ivy onto the coffin. There was a large number of floral tributes [and] two sprays of flowers from his grandchildren." (Wells Journal - Friday 13 May 1932)

The RAOB is the Royal Antediluvian Order of Buffaloes. This philanthropic organisation founded in 1822 supported people in need. Initially it operated an orphanage and then supplied six ambulances during the Great War. After the war, these became the first public ambulances in Britain.

Joseph Trenchard at war

There are scant but confusing details of Joseph's service during the war. The Wells Journal provides some information at the time of his death in February 1917 saying:

KILLED ACTION. Another Wellensian in the person of Pte Jos. Trenchard of the 3/4 Somerset Light Infantry, has given his life for his country… He had taken part in the recent fighting in Mesopotamia and an official notice from the War Office states he was killed in action on February 4th. Deceased, who was 20 years of age, was the eldest son of Mr. and Mrs. Trenchard of Priory-place, St. John-street. For some time he worked at Messrs. Ways and Co., and later at St. Cuthbert's Paper Works. Early in the war, he enlisted in the Somersets and was in camp at Cheddar for some months. His father is at present in France in a Labour Battalion, and a brother is serving with the Somerset R.H.A. in Egypt"

He died near Basra in modern day Iraq and his name appears on the Commonwealth War Graves' cemetery near that city; one of the cemeteries desecrated in 2013. This memorial commemorates more than 40,500 members of the Commonwealth forces who died in Mesopotamia between 1914 and August 1921 and whose graves are not known.

The War Graves Commission's records show that at the time he was with the 1/4th Hampshire regiment as does his medal card held by the National Archives recording a posthumous Victory Medal. However, all but one of the entries in the Wells Journal's Role of Honour says he was part of the 3/4th Somerset Light Infantry (SLI). The one exception from May 1916 shows him as being attached to the Hampshire Regiment as part of the Iraq Expeditionary Force. It is unclear why he joined the Hampshire Regiment who had arrived in Basra on 18th March 1915 as part of the 33rd Indian Brigade. They remained in Mesopotamia and Persia for the rest of the war.

General Maude, commander of the joint British / Indian forces in Mesopotamia launched a major offensive in December 1916 intended to capture Baghdad. A diversionary attack on Kut fixed the Ottoman Army there while the majority of Maude's force advanced through the desert on the opposite side of the Tigris. It was during this advance that Joseph Trenchard died. The advance was successful as Baghdad was taken on 11 March 1917 – five weeks after Joseph's death.

In July 1918, Father Morton recalled Joseph's life in Wells at the funeral of another former Scout:

"TRIBUTE TO DEAD SCOUT. The funeral took place at Wells Cemetery afternoon of William Edward Phipps, Wells young man, who was run down by a train, and instantaneously killed the Great Western Railway at the Severn Tunnel Junction early Saturday morning. Deceased, who was 19 years of age, took zealous interest the Boy Scout movement when Wells being the first boy join the 1st Wells Troop, and afterwards acting Assistant Scoutmaster of the troop.

"A companion, Joe Trenchard, was Patrol Leader of the Stags. I want you to honour his memory also, for he gave his life for our country, falling in battle in the marshes of Mesopotamia, and his grave is beyond our reach." (Wells Journal - Friday 19 July 1918)

THE WELSFORD - VINCENT FAMILY

The wider Welsford family had many members living in Wells during the lifetimes of the men who fought in the Great War. Three Welsfords appear on the Roll of Honour, as does Joseph Vincent who was related by marriage.

William Welsford Snr (1849-1929)

This Welsford family are descended from Giles (b 1816) and Sarah Welsford (b 1818) from Crediton, Devon. He was a Cordwainer (shoemaker). In the late 1840s, they moved to Bristol where Giles died in 1875. William (b 1849) is missing from the 1881 census, but the most likely candidate was a single man living in Moss Side Manchester working as a 'foreman tailor'.

By May 1883, he was in Wells and married Tamar Cook who had been a servant at the County Lunatic Asylum in 1871 and a cook at the Workhouse in 1881. For the rest of his life, William Snr. worked as an upholsterer. It is not clear whether he was in business 'on his own account' or if he was an employee of one of the firms, advertising upholstery services. In the 1880s, William played rugby football for a team called 'the Arabs' and by 1890 was acting as an umpire (referee) in local matches.

By 1891, William and Tamar were living in Ethel Street, Wells with two sons - Kenrick (b 1884) and Ernest George (b 1889), a daughter – Eleanor (b 1886) and William's niece – Elizabeth Fogg (b 1872) who worked as a paper sorter at Wookey

Mill. She had been part of the Welsford household in Bristol in 1871. A third son, named William John arrived in 1894. All three sons served in the Great War as did the Eleanor's husband Joseph Vincent.

William and Tamar rented their home in Ethel Street, something that bought periods of great uncertainty if an owner decided to sell. For example in January 1920, William and Tamar's home went up for sale. The adverts give a clear idea of their accommodation:

"Wells *Messrs, Bowring and Palmer son are instructed to offer for SALE BY AUCTION at the "Railway" Hotel, Wells, on TUESDAY, 17th February, 1920, at 7 o'clock in the evening … in Lots, the Four Desirable Freehold Dwelling houses, situated and being Nos. 1 to 4, Muriel Terrace, Alfred Street, in the In-Parish of St. Cuthbert, Wells, viz.*
Lot I. —the Desirable Freehold Dwelling house, with the Gardens thereto belonging, situate and being No. I, Muriel Terrace, Alfred Street, Wells, now occupied by Mr. Welsford, who holds same on a weekly tenancy at the low gross annual rental of £14 6s. 6d, the owner paying outgoings." (Around £520 in 2017 prices.)

Despite these sales, William remained in Muriel Terrace until his death in aged 80. His obituary from the Wells Journal (Friday 1 February 1929) read:

"SUDDEN DEATH AT WELLS. OLD AGE PENSIONER'S COLLAPSE IN The death occurred with much suddenness on Friday afternoon of Mr. Wm. Welsford (80), a retired upholsterer, who resided with his son. Mr. W. Welsford, at Muriel Terrace, Alfred Street. Deceased left his home about twenty past three on Friday afternoon to go to the Post Office in Priory Road to draw his old age pension. On reaching the Office, deceased complained of feeling unwell, and sat in a chair. He suddenly fell back, and before medical aid could be summoned, passed away.

His death was the subject of an inquest which was held at the Police Office on Monday afternoon … Annie Welsford and wife of Wm. Welsford, gardener of 1 Muriel Terrace. Alfred Street gave evidence of identification and said her father-in-law lived with her. He was retired upholsterer, and was 80 years of age. He was an old age pensioner. He had been ill for about a month, and had been attended by Dr Mullins. He had to get his pension on Friday. He left home about twenty past three to go to Priory Office. As he was feeling very unwell, she suggested going to get the pension for him. Deceased, however, said he was well enough to go. He was not feeling well in the morning and he had some bread and milk for dinner, but took only a little of what was put before him. He coughed and could not swallow his food very well and she thought he was weaker. … Dr Mullens of Wells said he had attended the deceased on four occasions—twice before Christmas and twice since—for a cough. Deceased came to his Surgery on Tuesday, January 22nd for some more medicine. He examined his throat and neck and found a hard lump, which he took be to a malignant growth. He was very deaf and he did not tell him anything about it. He intended seeing his son and to explain the case to him. Unfortunately, he had not seen the son. … The growth, accounted for the difficulty in swallowing and the cough. The growth was a malignant disease of the gullet. In his opinion, death was due to heart failure, caused by the cough by reason of the carcinoma of the gullet. The Coroner returning a verdict in accordance with the medical evidence … given by Dr Mullins.

The Funeral took place on Wednesday afternoon at the Wells Cemetery, the Rev. E. B. Cook officiating. The mourners were as follows: Mr K Welsford and Mr. W. J. Welsford (sons); Mrs. E Vincent (daughter); Mrs. G. Welsford (daughter' in-law) Mrs. L. Brooks (niece), Cheddar; .Messrs. R Welsford J. Welsford, G. E. Welsford, R. Vincent and Miss Queenie Welsford (grandchildren); There was a large number of beautiful floral tributes from the following —Wife and family; sister-in-law; Dick, Joe and George; Queenie and Bernard; Keene and Christina. Elizabeth Vincent; Emma Stephens; Mrs. L. Brooks, Cheddar; Mr. and Mrs. H. Hoskins and family; Mr. and Mrs. W. J. Brown; Mrs. King.

Tamar died in 1931. The Wells Journal reported

"Mrs. Tamar Amesbury Welsford aged 82 of 1 Muriel Terrace, Alfred Street, Wells, died in the Wells Cottage Hospital, on Saturday, from heart failure and shock caused by a fracture of the left femur through accidentally falling to the ground in her house. Deceased had resided with her son for the past 10 years, and until September nth was in fairly good health. On that date she slipped whilst walking from one room to another and sustained a fracture of the left femur. She was taken to the Cottage Hospital, where she died on Friday last. An inquest was held at the Cottage Hospital on Monday evening and was conducted Mr. W. G. Burroughs, Coroner for the district sitting without jury.

Anna Welsford, wife of William John Welsford, of 1, Muriel Terrace, Alfred-street, gave evidence of identification and said her mother-in-law was the widow of William Welsford, an upholsterer. The deceased had been living with her for the past ten years. She was 82 of age and was quite all right in her mind. She suffered from rheumatism and was crippled in her hands but not in her legs. She enjoyed fairly good health.

 On September 11th she came downstairs at 8.15 a.m. During the night, she was not very well, having complained of pains in her stomach. After the children had gone to school that morning her mother-in-law got up to go out of doors and fell down near the back door, said she was in the kitchen and heard deceased fall down. She ran out and saw her lying on her side. She could not get up. She called her husband, who assisted her to get deceased on to the sofa. Her husband went for Dr. Mullins. In reply to the Coroner, witness said there was no step or obstruction on the floor. It was stone floor. It was not polished. Afterwards deceased told her that she turned giddy and fell. She often turned giddy and felt taint. Deceased was removed to the Cottage Hospital.

Dr George Edward Mullins, of Wells, said he had attended the deceased for some years for various complaints, including rheumatism, dyspepsia, heart weakness and senile decay. On September 11th at about 10 a.m. he received a message asking him to call at Mrs. Welsford's. He called and found deceased lying on a couch suffering from a fracture of the neck of the right lemur and shock. He advised hospital treatment and she was removed to the Cottage Hospital by the Ambulance Brigade She had the usual treatment for a fractured femur but she never really got over the shock of the accident and died in her sleep on the morning of the 19th., Deceased's heart was old and feeble and in his opinion death was due to heart failure and shock cause by a fractured femur. Deceased told him that she slipped down.

The Coroner, in returning a verdict in accordance with the medical evidence said he was sorry deceased had shortened her days by this fall. He was quite satisfied that it was unavoidable. When people of this age do fall, it is a serious matter, and so often proves fatal. He expressed his sympathy with the sons in their bereavement."

Kenrick Welsford (1884-1946)

Kenrick, born on 12th February 1884 in Wells, was William and Tamar's eldest child. His full name recorded on the birth certificate was Kenrick William Harry Blizzard Welsford although many variants occur in the press and elsewhere. He was educated at Wells Central School and by the 1901 census was a 'cabinet maker'. By 1911, he was an assistant at Messrs Ways and Co. This was a family-run grocery business with a shop in the High Street, a thriving delivery business to private households and contracts to supply the Workhouse with groceries, butter, cheese, bacon, milk and coal. These workhouse contracts were renewed annually using highly competitive tendering process. The business introduced 'early closing' arrangements in 1908. 'Early closing' against the standards of the age meant the shop could close at 7.30 pm on Mondays, Tuesdays, Thursdays and Fridays. We do not know where in the business Kenrick worked nor whether this bought him into contact with Joseph Trenchard who worked there for a time.

In 1909, Kenrick married Mabel Gertrude Pollard (b 1881), the daughter of a tailor's cutter and originally from Fishponds, Bristol. She was 'in service' in 1901 and had a son Richard Pollard in 1907 who moved with her to Wells. Later he was known as Richard Welsford. In time, Kenrick and Mabel had two further sons Kenrick Joseph William (b 1910) and George E A (b 1913).

In the Edwardian era Kenrick was a noted athlete, often competing on behalf of the Mendip Harriers in both long distance marathons and sprints of 100 yards, as well as playing soccer.

Within a month of the start of the war, three Welsford men were amongst the 115 men who responded to the Mayor's call for volunteers for the newly formed Special Constabulary. These 'specials' allowed fit young policemen to join the armed forces. Kenrick became the subleader for Section 4 responsible for policing the Southover and Silver Street areas. The members of the section included his brother, William Welsford and Frederick Trenchard.

Kenrick joined the Welsh Regiment on 7th December 1915. He left the army on 28th August 1918, as he was *'No longer physically fit for service'*. The Wells Journal on 7th September 1917 reported that:

"Wounded —News has been received by Mrs Welsford, of St. Andrew-street, that her husband, Private K. Welsford, the Welsh Regiment, has been wounded, and at present is well cared for in a hospital at Oxford. Mr. Welsford, before joining up, was assistant at Ways and Co.,

High-street, and in letter to Mr. Bown, says:—"My right forearm was shattered, and there was a large wound, so it was either my arm or my life; I was taken out and the job done within 24 hours". It will be remembered that his brother, Pte. E. G. Welsford was killed in action in August last year."

The available records do not say exactly where the injury took place or what his role in the Welsh Regiment was at the time. For a period between his return to service after his injury and his formal discharge on 28th September 1918, he was at the Welsh Regiment Central Depot.

In January 1918, Lieut. R. Granville Harris, officer commanding the Wells Detachment of the 3rd Battalion, Somerset Volunteer Regiment, entertained the members of the Detachment and number of personal friends to dinner at the White Hart Hotel. In his speech, he said *"he should also like to mention Pte. K Welsford (applause), who had done so much, and had lost his right arm in one of the engagements. He was one of their members, and now he was back again he was still taking an active interest in his old detachment".*

What was he to do next? Making good use of the help available under 'King's National Roll' scheme, Kenrick secured work with the General Post Office. This scheme celebrated the contribution of good employers who found work for disabled ex-servicemen. By the end of 1919, 9,524 firms had taken on 89,619 disabled ex-servicemen. The number of disabled ex-service men registered as shown as unemployed on the registers of the Employment Exchanges in Great Britain on 11th June, 1920, was 19,235, compared with 35,079 in December 1919 – a fall of 45% in just 6 months. The scheme remained in operation until the Disabled Persons (Employment) Act 1944, established specialist services for all working-age people with disabilities. The Disability Discrimination Act 1995 and the Equality Act 2010, in turn, replaced this legislation. During the inter-war years, many employers were proud to display plaques issued by the Ministry of Labour recognising their commitment to ex-servicemen with disabilities.

In March 1920, Kenrick's rented home suffered a similar fate to that of his father. The Wells Journal published a sale notice relating to his home. It read:

"Important Sale of Conveniently Situated and Well-built MODERN FREEHOLD DWELLING-HOUSES. MESSRS. COLLINS & SONS have been favoured with instructions to SELL AUCTION at the Mermaid Hotel, Wells, on MONDAY, the 8th MARCH, 1920, at 8 o'clock in the Evening, the undermentioned Valuable Freehold Dwelling houses, viz.: …

LOT 4. —All that substantially built and convenient Messuage or Dwelling house situate and being No. 27, St. Cuthbert Street, Wells, containing Parlour or Sitting room fitted with 2 Cupboards. Hall, Kitchen with 3 Cupboards, back yard with Coal House, Furnace House and flushed w.c., Stairs and 2 good Bedrooms, occupied Mr. Welsford weekly tenant. Gas and Corporation Water laid on. …

The whole of the foregoing are let to good tenants at very low rental, and offer a rare opportunity to either investors or parties desirous of buying good newly built modern houses for their own occupation. To view, apply to the respective Tenants, and for further particulars to the Auctioneers Little Burcott House, Wells, or to MR. S. F. GOODALL, Solicitor, Wells. February 18th. 1920."

After the war, Kenrick became a 'rural postman' delivering mail to Priddy; entailing a walk of about 15 miles each day. He used a special device that allowed him to hold a bundle of letters on his artificial hand while posting them with his 'good' hand. He was an active trade unionist representing postal staff in Wells, and working people more widely.

His contribution to civic life went wider and endured until his death. In total, the Wells Journal devoted over 50,000 words to Kenrick, much but not all of it relating to his work as a City Councillor. He was defeated when he first stood for election as a Labour Party candidate in 1921 but persevered until he was was successful in 1932. Among the issues that attracted his attention and support were:

• High Quality affordable public housing in the age of 'Homes fit for heroes'

• Municipal sports facilities including football pitches, track facilities and public swimming pools

• Good quality playgrounds for young children

• Good conditions including pensions, paid holidays and hospital league contributions for Council employees

• Support for the League of Nations Association

• Publicly funded apprenticeships

• Disarmament

• Easing the harsh application of the Unemployment Act 1934 – that limited benefit payments in many circumstances

• Equal Pay for women in public services

• Removing political and other restrictions on public servants, including postal workers

These interests reflect elements in the Labour Party's national programme in the interwar years. Labour's landslide election victory led to the Attlee Government in August 1945 – just ten months before Kenrick's sudden death.

His wider interests include the long list of local organisations where he offered support or active participation including:

- The local and Regional Labour Party organisations
- The Union of Post Office Workers
- Local and regional trades councils
- Ratepayers Association
- The Comrades' Club which became part of the British Legion in 1921
- Wells Cooperative Society
- League of Nations Union
- Loyalty League
- Workers Educational Association
- War Pensions Committee
- Wells City Football Club
- Wells City Supporters Club
- Wells Advertising Association

Clearly, he was a highly committed, perhaps highly driven man focused on the ideals of the wider socialist family of the Labour Party, the local Cooperative Society and trade unions. His commitment was uncomfortable for other Council members who saw him as unruly and hostile to the traditional ways of doing business. In particular, they disliked the bitter rows he provoked in full council about decisions taken by Council committees that were not open to the public.

He died suddenly in June 1946. The Wells Journal reported this on 7th June 1946:

"SUDDEN DEATH MR. K. WELSFORD SENIOR CITY COUNCILLOR ONLY LABOUR MEMBER. We regret to record the death occurred suddenly this (Thursday) morning of Mr. Kenrick Wm. H. B. Welsford of 3 Kenyon Road, Wells, aged 62 years. Mr. Welsford was about as usual on Wednesday evening and the news of his passing comes as a great shock to his many friends in the City. Senior Councillor of Wells he attended Monday evening's meeting of the Council and took his usual share in the discussions. He was seen in his garden late on Wednesday night and was then in his usual state of health. It appears that at about 5 this morning Mr. Welsford awoke complained of pains in the chest. Mrs Welsford went downstairs to make her husband a cup of tea and he followed her downstairs. Within a few minutes of returning to bed, Mr. Welsford passed away.

Mr. Welsford, who was a native of Wells, was educated at the Central School. Leaving school took up a position as assistant at Messrs Ways and Co; grocer joined the Welch Regiment and served in France, losing his arm. Upon his discharge in 1919 joined the staff of the Wells Post as an auxiliary postman and was was appointed rural postman and remained such until his retirement las He was one of the original members of the Wells British Legion branch Wells, previously being associated with the Comrades Club in Broad Street.

He first sought municipal honours in 1921 but was defeated. He persevered through a series of defeats until he was returned unopposed in a bye-election in 1932. ... At subsequent elections he was "returned unopposed and last November (1945) when he had to again come to the electors he topped the poll with 1.591 votes, 16 candidates being in the field...

Mr. Welsford's career to the last has been marked sterling work and on many occasions, he has been a lone voice. A zealous critic at times of the Council's policy he faced a good deal of opposition ... He was connected with many organisations, including the Wells Advertising Association, the Wells Football Supporters Club, of which he was vice-chairman, and the Wells City F. C., serving on the Management Committee. Much sympathy is extended Mrs Welsford and her family."

The funeral took place four days later and was reported in the Wells Journal (14th June 1946):

"THE LATE MR. K. WELSFORD CITY COUNCILLORS AMONG THE MANY MOURNERS. Members of Wells City Council and representatives of many organisations with which he has been associated, attended the funeral on Monday morning of the late Mr. Kenrick Wm. H. B. Welsford, senior councillor of Wells, whose sudden death at the age of 62 years was recorded in our last issue. The news of K Welsford's death on Thursday morning of last week came as a great surprise to the people of Wells, as the previous day he was about the city apparently in his usual health.

He was a man who devoted himself whole-heartedly to public service. Even the claim of municipal work made upon his time did not deter him from coming forward to serve the city in other ways. He was well known for his political enthusiasm, for the help rendered Wells soccer and for his interest in the British Legion. He also served on the committees of the Wells Advertising Association and League of Nations Union. Other organisations received his ready support and cooperation, and he will be missed by many who had shared and valued his help and friendship.

The body was conveyed to the Church of S.S. Joseph and Teresa on Sunday evening, where it rested overnight. The Rev. Father Foran officiated at Requiem Mass on Monday morning, and also at the interment at Wells Cemetery. The coffin was covered with the Union Jack.

The mourners were : Mrs. Kenrick Welsford, widow; Richard, Joseph and George, sons; Mrs. Joseph Vincent, sister ; Mr. William Welsford, brother ; Mrs. Richard Welsford, Mrs. Joseph Welsford, Mrs. George Welsford, daughters-in-law ; Mr. Joseph Vincent, brother in-law Mrs. William Welsford, sister-n-law ; Mrs. Martin, sister-in-law ; Mrs. Herbert Mallows, Miss Christine Welsford, Miss Barbara Vincent, nieces ; Mr. Bernard Vincent, Mr. Kenrick Welsford, nephews ; Miss Agnes Vincent, cousin ; Mr. and Mrs. H. Hoskins, Mr. and Mrs. W. Brock (Bristol), Mr. J. C. Toomer, Mr. and Mrs. G. Froud, Mrs. Bernard Vincent, Mr. Ernest Lane, friends.

The City Council attended in State, but the Mayor (Ald. H. Sealey) was unable to be present, being away from home. With the Deputy Mayor (Ald. H. W. Reakes) were Aldermen G. W. Hippisley and F. P. Cocks, Councillors C. H. Barnes. E. E. Sheldon, W. Gadd, H. Paul, T. H. Reeves, W. G. Purchase, E. de M. Kippax and Mrs. Melrose, with the Town Clerk, Mr.

H. J. Dodd. The deputy Mayor's mace was draped. Wells Branch of the British Legion was represented by Major J. L. Portal, D. (President), Mr. J. Hawes (chairman), Capt. E. W. Harper (secretary), R. Packer, H. Swain, E. Western and Standard-bearer A. Loxton. British Legion members also acted as bearers, Messrs. J. Hawes, E. Cook, A. Radford and E. Vincent.

Mr. F. J. Shatwell (President), Mr. P. A. Hole (Vice-President), and Mr. H. C. Angel (secretary) represented the Wells Labour Party, many members being among the congregation. Others present were Mr. J. P. Underdown (Chairman, Wells Advertising Association), Messrs. W. Palmer and A. C. Cook (Wells and District Trades Council). Mr. E. E. Sheldon (vice-chairman) and Mr. H. G. Hann, Wells City F.C., Messrs. J. Innes and H. C. Baker (Wells Football Supporters' Club), Section-Leader F. Sampson (Wells N.F.S.) [National Fire Service].

Wells Post Office Staff was represented by Postmen W. H. Pritchard, J. Watts, A. Savage and W. Turner. Mr, A. M. Sandover (former Head Postmaster) was also present. Others attending were Mr. S. F. Goodall (Clerk, Wells Burial Board), Dr. J. McGarvey, Mrs. Van Eyken, Mr. A. L. Van Eyken, Misses A. and L. Van Eyken, Miss Campbell, Miss Reakes, Mrs. Evans. Mrs. Hamilton, Mrs. Bishop, Mrs. Young, Mr. and Mrs. S. Parker, Miss Smith, Mrs. C. Francis, Mr. and Mrs. C.Seal, Mrs. McCabe, Mrs. 'Powell, Mr. and Mrs. G. Salmon, Mrs. Sparks, Mrs. Hopton, Mrs. Wills, Mrs. A. Stevens, Mrs. K. Mapstone, Mrs. E. Board, Miss Board, Mr. and Mrs. H. Cook, Mr. H. C. Kenney, Mr. G. Hecht, Mr. J. Trenchard, Mr. W. V. P. Lewis. Mr. V. J. Butler, Mr. F. Clark, Mrs. H. C. Angel, Mr G. Bishop, Mr. A. Parsons and others.

Kenrick's Family life

At the start of the Great War, Kenrick had three sons - Richard (b 1906), Kenrick Joseph William (b 1910) and George Edward (b 1913).

Richard, the eldest, was single and living with his parents in 1939 and working as as postman – driver. He married Mary Gilbert, of Glastonbury in the spring of 1942 by which time he was in the Royal Engineers' postal section. After the end of the war, he returned to Wells and the GPO. Shortly afterwards in spring 1946, he left the GPO and set up in business in Glastonbury. In the post war years, he was a prominent member of the British Legion and maintained an interest in sport as a member of the County Cricket Club, vice-president of the Glastonbury Football Supporters' Club, and bowls. He died in 1968.

Kenrick Joseph William, the second son, was born in April 1910. He was living with his parents in 1939 and worked as a Clerk to a Surveyors Draughtsman. Later, in December 1939 he married Elneth Davies Foster at the Pro Cathedral in Bristol. He died at Hounslow, near London, in 1966.

George Edward Anthony, the youngest son was born in 1913. He married Katherine Brock, daughter of Mr. and Mrs. H. Brock, of Kingsdown Parade, Bristol at the Pro-Cathedral, Bristol, in November 1940 ... *"The bridegroom was formerly employed as a draughtsman at Messrs. Sheldon's, Wells, and was resident in Cheltenham. They spent their honeymoon at Minehead."* He died at Cheltenham in 1990.

Ernest was born in 1889. By the time of the 1911 Census, he was working as a cheese porter. He married Ellen E King in spring 1913. Their daughter, Gwendoline Mary Eleanor was born in 1914.

Ernest joined the army in April 1916 served in the 6th Battalion, Somerset Light Infantry. The battalion was involved in the Battle of the Somme. In August 1916, they took apart in the Battles of Delville Wood and Pozieres.

On 15th September 1916 the Wells Journal reported:

"ROLL OF HONOUR. We regret to have to record the death of another Wellensian in action in the person of Pte. E. G. Welsford, of the' 3rd Somerset L.I. Deceased, who was 27 years of age, was the second son of Mr. W. Welsford, of Muriel-terrace, and had only seen five months' service. After three months' training, he was sent across to France, and was attached to the 1st Wilts Regt. He was early in the fighting and quite recently, official intimation was received of his having been wounded. He appears to have recovered rapidly for he was with his regiment on August 24th, and was killed in the heavy fighting. The late Pte. Welsford, who prior to joining up, was employed at Messrs. Ways and Sons' cheese stores, leaves a widow and one child, for whom much sympathy is felt."

In 1918 and 1919, the family arranged for memorial notices in the Wells Journal:

Killed in action, August 24th, 1916, Pte. E G Welsford, Somerset L.I.
"Two years have passed since that sad day,
When we loved was called away;
His smiles we missed, his welcome face,
 None can fill his vacant place.
 Not dead to those who loved him,
 Not lost, but gone before."
 By his sorrowing Widow and loving Child. R.I.P.

WELSFORD
Killed action, August 24th, 1916. Pte E. G. Welsford, Somerset L.I.
He little thought when leaving home,
That would never return
And now lies in a soldier's grave,
And leaves us all to mourn.
Calmly took his place,
He fought and died for Britain,
And the honour of his race.
His sorrowing Father, Mother, Brothers, and Sister.
R.I.P.

IN MEMORIAM Welsford —In loving Memory Pte. Ernest George Welsford,
22615, E. Company, 3rd Batt., S.L.I. Killed in Action August 24th, 1916.
Ever remembered by his Sorrowing Mother and Father.
Days of sadness still come over us,
Tears in silence often flow
Memory keeps him ever near us,
Though he died three years ago
R.I.P.

In June 1939, the Journal reported that *"the wedding took place at the Roman Catholic Church of Miss Gwendoline May Welsford, only daughter of Mrs. and the late Mr. E. G. Welsford, of Wells, and Mr. Ethelbert Mallows, elder son of Mr. and Mrs. W. Mallows, of South View, Burcott Road. The Rev. Father McEnery officiated, and Miss Mellor was at the organ. The bride, who was given away by her uncle, Mr. J. Vincent, was dressed in pale pink figured crepe-de-chine, with Juliet cap of flowers to match. … A reception was held at The City Cafe and was attended by about 40 guests. The honeymoon is being spent at Weymouth."*

Gwendoline died at Glastonbury in January 2014 just after her 100th birthday.

William Welsford (1893 - 1977)

William John was born in spring 1893 and baptised at St Cuthbert's church. In 1901, the family were living in Southover. In 1907 and 1908, William John took leading roles in the annual spring entertainments at the Catholic School. In 1907, he played Dick (a hunchback) in the play, 'The Earl of Dorincourt'. In 1908, he played Thomas in 'A Spoiled Child Little Pickle'. His co-stars included Ena and Stellar Coggan, and William Hugh and Kathleen MacMahon. In 1911, William John was in Muriel Terrace and working as an under-gardener on domestic gardens.

His military records have not survived and his service was not mentioned in the Wells Journal suggesting that he was not in the front line.

He married Annie Eliza King in autumn 1921. She was born in 1894 and by 1911 was working as a domestic servant at Eastcourt in Wookey. This was in the household of Alfred Thrale Perkins, a retired Army Colonel. In autumn 1924, they had a daughter, Christina M A. Welsford.

Annie and William appear in the 1939 Register. He was working as a gardener and she as a cleaner. Two restricted entries may have related to Christina and a sibling. In 1949, the Wells Journal reported a domestic incident involving Annie Welsford:
"Muriel Terrace Disturbance ASSAULT CASES DISMISSED Wells City Magistrates were occupied for some while on Tuesday in hearing cases of assault brought by residents of Muriel Terrace, in Alfred-street. William Parkin, of 5, Muriel Terrace, pleaded not guilty to assaulting Annie Welsford, of No. 1, Muriel Terrace. Mrs. Welsford pleaded not guilty to an assault on Mr. Parkin.

Mr. C. Wyndham Harris, for Mrs. Welsford, said this was more than a neighbour's quarrel. Mr. Parkin was Mrs. Welsford's landlord and he said witnesses would be called to prove that Mr. Parkin was an oppressive and bad tempered man, and that they were shocked at the treatment he had meted out this poor, unfortunate woman." … As there was conflicting evidence, the magistrates dismissed both cases.

Joseph Vincent (1888 – 1949)

His name appears in different forms on various public documents, often with the middle names of Alfred and / or Sargent. He was born in Marnhull, Dorset to Georgina Vincent. No father's name appears on the birth certificate. In 1891 and 1901, Joseph appears as a 'border' with the Moore family of Marnhull.

In 1905, he moved to Wells and in spring, 1910 married Eleanor Welsford (b 1886). Thus, he became a brother-in-law to Ernest and Kenrick Welsford. He was a public-spirited man. In 1911, he competed in a contest for the best-illuminated display for the coronation of George V and won five Guineas – about £500 in 2018 values. In 1912, he intervened in a street fight in Southover to rescue a woman being attacked.

Joseph and Eleanor had three children - Ralph W A Vincent (1910), Bernard (1918) and Barbara (1931). Each was talented in various fields. Ralph won second prize of 15s (75p), now equivalent to around £125 in a competition for the 'best essay entitled 'How I can best protect Wild Birds'. Ralph played King Arthur in the 1926 'entertainment' provided by the children of the Catholic School.

Joseph probably served as a driver in the Royal Field Artillery during the Great War but no further details of his service are available. After the war, he returned to Wells. He was a private man rarely mentioned in the press, although clearly a 'public spirited man as a member of the British Legion, the Wells Carnival Committee and the Knights of St Columba.

Joseph appears to have worked as a baker for most of his life. In 1930, he applied for a licence to sell ice creams from a barrow in the Market Place. This was granted subject to a payment three shillings a week (about £25 in 2018 prices); the purity of the product; and the condition of the premises where it was made. The notice of his death in January 1949 in the Wells Journal mentions that *"he was for many years an ice cream seller"* but this seems to have been a subsidiary and seasonal occupation. In 1943, he was a grocery van driver.

The Wells Journal reported that the mourners at his funeral in 1949 were Mrs Evens of the Catholic School, 'friends at Sun and Full Moon Inns' and many relatives from the extended Welsford and Vincent families.

In 1936, Barbara Vincent was part of the team from the Sun Inn that entered a tableau called 'Say it in flowers' in that year's carnival. In February 1939, she took part in a Dancing Competition held at the Y.M.C.A. at Colston Street, Bristol, in aid the Blind. She gained one certificate and one entry for semi-finals at Birmingham. In the following month, she gained a 'highly commended' award at a festival of leisure time pursuits' held at Wells Town Hall.

In 1943 the Bath Chronicle reported *that 'Sgt. B. Vincent, S.L.I., second son of Mr and Mrs J. Vincent of Wells, and Miss V. Vaughan, second daughter of Mr and Mrs J Vaughan, of 35, Beechen Cliff Place Holloway, Bath, were married on Saturday at St. Alpheges Church, Oldfleld Park, by Father Kelly. The bride was given in marriage by her father and the best man was Mr L. Aldred. After the service, reception was held at the bride's home. Violet worked in a clothing factory and her father was a grocery van driver'.* They settled in Bath where Bernard died in the winter of 1989. Barbara married in 1952.

Ralph who became a member of the Duke of Cornwall's Light Infantry and was injured while serving in France in 1940. In the spring 1945, he married Violet A Wood and they settled in her home town of Hove. He died in 1971.

CUTHBERT SHIRLEY WINSLOW (1893 – 1917)

Cuthbert Shirley Winslow joined the army in Wells while showing his town of residence as Ramsgate where his brother was a Catholic priest. His links with Wells were were slight but he was remembered by the people who commissioned on the church's roll of honour. He came from a wealthy well-educated prominent family. He did not become a Catholic until 1911 and died in action in 1917.

Cuthbert's early life

Cuthbert Shirley Winslow was the third son of Edward Jnr and Mary Winslow born at Wandsworth, London, in 1893.

His grandfather, also Edward, born in 1802 was one of the two 'Masters in Lunacy' appointed by the Commissioners in Lunacy, established under the Lunacy Act 1845. Their role was to oversee asylums and the welfare of mentally ill people, and report to the Poor Law Commissioners (in the case of workhouses) and to the Lord Chancellor. The Masters acted as guardians of lunatics, administered their property and made inquiries into the state of mind of persons alleged to be insane. This was a high profile role requiring a strong legal training, experience and great sensitivity.

Edward's mother died in 1844 when he was 13. In 1851, Edward Jnr was living in London's fashionable Torrington Square, Bloomsbury with his widowed father, seven siblings and four servants. He was a student at Kings College, London and went on to become a successful lawyer.

Edward Snr appears to have married again in January, 1865 when the Morning

PIVOTAL MEMBERS OF THE CATHOLIC COMMUNITY IN WELLS

Bishop Clifford of Clifton (1823 -1893)
(Source Creative Commons, Wikipedia)

Rev Thomas William Morton (1862–1945)
Pictured during his time in Canada.
(Courtesy: Memorable Manitobans)

Rev. Mother, Convent Wells
Original photograph by Philips
© Wells & Mendip Museum

CORPUS CHRISTI 1914 - 14TH JUNE

WARTIME SOLDIERS IN WELLS

The Somersets leaving for India, September 1914 from Tucker Street Station
(Picture Bert Phillips, courtesy Wells Railway Fraternity, Colin Price Collection)

Soldiers & Nurses at the Cedars Hospital in Wells
(Source – The Somerset Remembers Community Archive)

WELSFORD FAMILY

Back row: **Ellen** (in her nurse's uniform), **Ernest, William and Kenrick**. **Front row: Tamar and William Snr**. The young child and the woman on the right are not known.
(Photograph courtesy of Mrs Lavina Parfitt, William's granddaughter.)

Ernest, Ellen and **Gwendoline** (born 19th December 1913) **Welsford** taken just before he left Wells 1916.
(Photograph courtesy of Mrs Lavina Parfitt, William's granddaughter.)

Left-RIght: **Ernest, William** and **Kenrick Welsford**
(Courtesy of Mrs Sheila Spencer, William's grand daughter)

MUTHU FAMILY

David and Margaret Muthu c1890
(Courtesy: Shelly Kapadia)

The Muthu children with their governess
(Courtesy: Cyrus P. Kapadia and the "Knowing more on Dr Muthu" Blog)

David, Margaret and Family c1900
(Courtesy: Shelly Kapadia)

Dr David Jacob Aaron Chowry–Muthu
(Courtesy of Shelly Kapadia, Granddaughter)

Leslie, Olive and Bernard Muthu on the right
(Courtesy: Shelly Kapadia)

Muthu family home on Portway, Wells
(Courtesy: Shelly Kapadia)

PEACE DAY 1919

Post Office staff – probably includes Kenrick Wellsford
(possibly back row, 3rd from the left)

Carnival float
(Courtesy Liz Mapstone)

Advertiser reported that *"On the 5 inst., at the British Legation, Brussels, the Rev. W. Drury, M.A., Chaplain U.M. the King of the Belgians, Edward Winslow, Esq., barrister-at-law, to Loetilia Champagne, second daughter of the late John Armstrong, Esq., Killclare, King's County, Ireland."* The Daily Telegraph & Courier noted that Edward Snr died in the autumn of 1880 at Brentford, Middlesex. In December 1903, the Daily Telegraph & Courier reported *"Deaths … On Dec 18 at 64 Mildmay Park. N., Loetilia Carrington Champagne Winslow. Widow of Edward Winslow Esq of Twickenham, Barrister at Law, formerly Master in Lunacy".*

By 1871, Edward Jnr was living alone in Chancery Lane, Liberty of the Rolls, Strand, London. He married Mary Agnes Charrington (b 1858) at Staines in 1887. Mary was the sister of John Charrington the master brewer who created a large national brewery company. Edward and Mary lived in Wandsworth and had three sons - Keith Frederick (b 1889), Leslie (b 1890) and Cuthbert (1893).

When Edward Jnr. retired in 1905, the family moved to Wroxall on the Isle of Wight. On 26th June 1909 the Isle of Wight County Press and South of England Reporter (26th June 1909) said *"Barrister's Death. Early Saturday morning, Mr. Edward Winslow, passed away at his residence 'Green Bank', after a brief illness. The deceased gentleman, who was in his seventy-ninth year, was formerly barrister in active and successful practice at the Chancery Bar. He, with Mrs. Winslow and family, settled in Wroxall about four years ago, and their acts of benevolence have been extensive. Mr. Winslow was present at both services at the Parish Church, where he was sidesman, on Sunday week, and was taken ill after evening service. The sad event was referred to in sympathetic terms at Sunday's services the Rev. C. P. Calvert, who is now in charge of the parish."*

Edward's death was a devastating blow for Cuthbert and Keith. After a long period of reflection, both decided to become Catholics. Following instruction by a priest at the London Oratory, they were received into the Church in 1910. Previously, Keith had thought seriously about joining the Orthodox Church.

In 1911, Keith was a guest at Ampleforth Abbey, the leading Catholic Public School in Yorkshire. Three years later, he entered the Novitiate at St Augustine's Abbey in Ramsgate, taking the name Bede on 1st April 1914.

Also in 1911, Cuthbert was a pupil at the Hawksyard Priory School near Rugely in Staffordshire run by the Dominicans. Their mother, Mary Winslow, was in Putney Heath with her brother, sister-in-law and their two daughters at the time of the 1911 Census. The household of five employed a housekeeper, butler, page, nurse and 10 other servants. Mary died in 1938 in Reading.

After leaving Hawksyard, Cuthbert next appears in Wells. In early 1916, shortly after conscription started, the Wells Journal reported:

'APPEALS WHICH FAILED Lieut. E. R. Wilmshurst informed the Tribunal that the appeals against the decisions refusing to exempt Edwin Fry. a worker at the Wilts United Dairies, of 32, St. Thomas street; Frank Edwin Sawyer, assistant superintendent the Pearl Assurance Company, 1 St. Cuthbert's terrace; Thomas Charles Bowles, a conscientious objector, of Broad-street; and Cuthbert Shirley Winslow, organist, 9 Chamberlain-street, came before the Appeal Tribunal Bath, on Friday, and were all dismissed. The Mayor said he attended the Bath sitting, and the cases took a very short time'. (Wells Journal, Friday 31 March 1916).

Owing to the sensitive nature of decisions about compulsory military service during the Great War, most of the records were destroyed in the 1920s. Cuthbert's military records show that although he enlisted in Wells, he listed his place of residence as Ramsgate; presumably giving Dom Bede's (his brother Keith) address.

Cuthbert at war

After the dismissal of Cuthbert's appeal, he joined the army. Initially he was part of the Gloucestershire Regiment but after a short while moved to the Royal Warwickshire Regiment as a member of the 11th (Service) Battalion as part of the 112th Brigade in the 37th Division. The regiment took part in the Battle of Ancre and Cuthbert Winslow died in action on 14th November 1916 aged 23.

His sacrifice is recorded on at least four memorials – SS Joseph and Teresa's Roll of Honour; Wells War Memorial; Wroxall (Isle of Wight) Parish War Memorial; and the Thiepval Memorial. This memorial commemorates more than 72,000 men of the British and South African forces who died in the Somme before 20 March 1918 without a known grave.

Cuthbert's family after the war - Leslie

Cuthbert's oldest brother, Leslie, was educated at Dover College. In December 1914, he was one of over 400 'Old Dovorians' in the forces. In all, 177 former pupils of the College died in action in the Great War.

Leslie was already in the army as a second lieutenant in the Royal Field Artillery when war broke out. By the end of August 1914, he was a full lieutenant and in October 1918, he became an acting Captain. On retirement he was granted the title Major (Brevet) – meaning that this was an honorary rank. He retired from the RA in July 1935. After 1939, he became a Temporary Lieutenant Colonel. He made several trips to the USA in the 1950s and died in April 1974, possibly in Florida.

Cuthbert's family after the war – Keith (known as Dom. Bede)

After his ordination in April 1914, Father Bede remained in Kent for the rest of his life. After visiting the Oriental College in Rome in 1924, he decided to devote his life to work and prayer for the reunion of Christendom. He soon began to elicit interest in his idea for a monastery for Christian re-union. Bede's many friends and supporters included Lord Halifax (a leading Conservative Minister) and Orthodox Christians from many traditions and Eastern rite Catholics.

In 1934, Bede became the parish priest of Minster as well as serving Catholics based at RAF Mansion. When a new community of nuns came to Minster in 1937 from St Walburga's Abbey, Eichstatt, Bavaria, ecumenism became an important part of their community's life.

By the early 1950s, Dom Bede was a well-known advocate, speaker and writer on Christian Unity frequently sharing public platforms with senior figures from other Christian denominations, including Dr Fisher, the Archbishop of Canterbury. In 1950, the Archbishop of Canterbury (and leader of the Anglican Union) presided at meeting on Christian Unity saying *'he was deeply concerned for co-operation and understanding between the Churches. The thing they had to obtain, by the Grace of God, was what a distinguished Catholic leader had described as civilised relations between all Christian denominations.'* The speakers at the meeting were Canon C. H. E. Smyth, of Westminster; Rev. J. Newton Flew, principal of Wesley House, Cambridge; an ex-moderator the Free Church Council, and Dom Bede Winslow O.S.B. representing the Catholic Church.

Dom Bede died suddenly on 30th October 1959 whilst at St Joseph's College, Beulah Hill in London where he was to attend a meeting to discuss his dream of a Monastery for reunion. Father Brochard Sewell writing in The Tablet described Bede as *'a very holy monk of quite exceptional personal charm who did good by wearing his habit always and everywhere.'*

MEN ABOUT WHOM WE HAVE LIMITED INFORMATION

Fredrick Chappell (1890 - 1970)

Frederick William Chappell was the son of Frederick and Amy Chappell who lived at 3 Ethel Street and was baptised at St Cuthbert's on 22nd October 1890.
Amy was originally from Bristol but in the 1881 census was as an attendant at the Coney Hatch Lunatic Asylum in Middlesex. At the time of her marriage in 1888 to Fredrick Chappell Snr, he was a butcher employed by Jas. White in Queen Street. Sometime before 1901, he became a Photographer's assistant but by 1911, Frederick and Fredrick William, were general labourers.

Tracing Frederick William Junior's army career is difficult. He enrolled in April 1915 and discharged in January 1916 as being 'sick'. He was a private in 19th London (St Pancras) Regiment. His discharge on grounds of being sick is vague – was the sickness the result of an injury or a serious illness unrelated to his army service? Presumably, he returned to the family home where his mother died in 1927 and his father in 1931. However being discharged as 'sick' would be consistent with the 1939 Register that shows him receiving an 'Army Disability pension' and living with his unmarried sister

Amy, at 44a Mill Street Wells. She was a 'rag sorter' at St Cuthbert's paper mill. Amy died in 1954 and Frederick in 1970 at Bristol.

Cyril Davis (unknown)

It is not possible to identify Cyril Davis or variants of this name in Wells, Somerset or Gloucestershire (including Bristol) with any certainty. The most likely candidate was living at 75 High Street who became a member of the Royal Army Medical Corps.

A Mr Cyril Davis, of Portway, Wells, was a cashier Parr's Bank in 1923. In August 1932, an MG. car driven by Mr Cyril Davis, of Frome, and formerly of the Westminster Bank, Wells, crashed into a wall near Hunters' Lodge, Priddy. He appears in the 1939 register living at Frome.

Martin Patrick Foley (1895 - 1944)

Martin Foley's links with Wells were tenuous. He seems to have been born around 1895 in Co. Sligo. He does not appear in the England and Wales 1901 Census. Nor was he part of the three Foley families living in Somerset in 1911 with close Irish associations.

He first appears in Somerset living at 19 Chamberlain Street, Wells and working at Wells Lunatic Asylum as an Attendant. In June 1916, Dr Stevens Pope, the Medical Superintendent of the Asylum, appealed to the Board of Control, who administered the conscription system locally, that nine men including Martin Foley were vital to the operation of the asylum. The Board recommended that seven should be exempt from conscription until 30th September whilst two others, including Martin Patrick Foley were not covered reports of the judgement.

This omission might be explained as Martin Foley's military records show he enlisted in February 1916 and became a corporal in No 3 battalion of the Royal Engineers. Martin Foley specialised in the cable systems known as 'airlines' used to communicate between Royal Flying Corps stations and the RGA gun positions. He remained in this specialism until the end of the war as the work moved from the RGA to the Royal Artillery (1917) and onto the Royal Engineers (1917).

On Christmas Eve 1917, Martin entered the 139th Field Ambulance Hospital but the reason is unknown. He left hospital in January 1918 when the 139th were close to Treviso in Italy. Prior to his discharge from the army in 1919, he was with the 81st Motor Airline Section. Ordinary 'airline sections' laid and serviced cable routes working from horse-drawn wagons, although Martin's unit used motor vehicles.

We hear nothing further of Martin Foley until he appears in the 1939 Register as an 'incapacitated patient' at the East Lancashire Homes in Park Lane, Salford. This was Broughton House opened in 1916 following an appeal by the East Lancashire branch of the British Red Cross aimed at easing the pressures on hospitals in the Manchester area. Why he went to Greater Manchester is not clear. Martin Foley died at the age of 49 in spring 1944.

William Jay (unknown)

It has not been possible to trace William Jay with an association with Wells in public records or newspapers.

Patrick Kelly (unknown)

It has not been possible to trace a Patrick Kelly to Wells. The nearest candidate of the right generation was living in Taunton in 1939 and working as an Aircraft Detail Fitter Skilled and Iron Moulder. There were some three and a half thousand people called Kelly in the forces in the Great War; only six of whom had any recorded association with Somerset and none with Wells.

William James Read (1883-1917)

William James Read was born at Blackhorn Weston in 1886. Buckhorn Weston is in the Blackmore Vale in North Dorset and about 4 miles from Wincanton. He was the fifth of the eight children of George and Anna Read. The family remained in Buckthorn Weston until the Edwardian period. By 1911, they were living at the Blacksmith Shop in Croscombe. His father was a Coach Builder Journeyman having been a wheelwright and Carpenter in earlier census returns. William worked as an Assurance Agent.

In the spring of 1911, William married Joanna Finn (b 1872) in Wells. She was the daughter of Josephi (Joseph) and Ellena (Ellen) Finn. Joanna was baptised at St Francis of Assisi Catholic Church in Notting Hill in West London. Her parents came from Limerick. Joanna appears in the 1881 Census but not in later years. It is unclear how William and Joanna met or where they lived at the time of their wedding.

William does not appear on the Wells War Memorial but features on the memorial at Worle, near Weston super Mere. This records the death of William James Read who was a private in 6th Battalion, Prince Albert's (Somerset Light Infantry), part of the 43rd Brigade of the 1st 4th (Light) Division. His birthplace was Blackthorn Weston and he enlisted at Weston-Super-Mare. He died in action on 9th April 1917.

He is one of 110 British and Canadian soldiers buried at the Tigris Lane Cemetery, near Arras in Pas de Calais. The Commonwealth War Graves Commission says that he was the *"son of George and Anna Read; husband of Johanna Read, of 32, Milton Green, Weston-super-Mare".* Milton Green is close to Worle.

THE HOME FRONT

Having looked at the Catholics who went to war, we must not neglect the contribution of those who remained in Wells to the 'national war effort'. Sadly, although their efforts were widely recognised, little has survived in detail, mostly in fragmentary references in the Wells Journal. Few of these references mention specific people.

Nor do we have any reliable records of the names of the Catholics living and worshiping in Wells in the early twentieth century. Consequently, this section offers a summary of the main ways in which people contributed to the war effort, with any specific information about the situation in Wells and the involvement of the catholic community drawn from the Wells Journal.

The major exception to this is the wealth of information (around 30,000 words devoted in the Wells Journal between 1914 and 1919) about the contribution of the Reverend Father Morton.

REVEREND FATHER THOMAS WILLIAM MORTON (1862 - 1943)

His contribution is best seen in the context of his life before he became the priest in charge at SS Joseph and Teresa, Wells in 1914 and what he did after he left in 1919.

Early Life

Thomas William Morton was born on 15 September 1862 in Boston, Lincolnshire, the first child of Thomas Naylor Morton (1816 - 1898) and Augusta Morton (1826 – 1902). He grew up in a Catholic family as Blessed John Henry Newman received his father, previously an Anglican clergyman, into the Catholic Church in 1853. As a married man, he could not become a Catholic priest.

By 1871, the Mortons, including Thomas and three younger brothers were living in Dalton in Furness in Cumbria. Both Thomas and Augusta were schoolteachers and the household included a 'visitor' whose occupation was 'priest's housekeeper'.

By 1881, the family were in Liverpool where Thomas Naylor Morton was a 'Munimentarian' employed by the Librarian of Liverpool Corporation. A 'Muniment of Title' is a legal term for a document, title deed or other evidence that indicates ownership of an asset. Keeping track of changes in property ownership was important in the rapidly growing city like nineteenth century Liverpool.

Thomas William was 18 years old and a boarder at the Catholic Institute (now St Edward's College) in Everton. After six years at the Catholic Institute, he entered the Society of Jesus on 7 September 1882 at Manresa Hall, Roehampton, near London. He remained there until 1886, when he went to St Mary's Hall, Stonyhurst at Clitheroe in Lancashire, for 3 years of philosophy (part of the Jesuit formation process), physics and astronomy.

From 1889, he spent 12 years as Science Master at Beaumont College, Old Windsor. The college dated from 1854 when the Society of Jesus bought it as a training college for Jesuit novices of the (then) English province. In October 1861, it became a Catholic boarding school for boys, with the title of St. Stanislaus College and as such was an important part of the growing 'Catholic public school' tradition in England. He remained a 'scholastic' member of the Society of Jesus, continuing his studies for the priesthood until he left the Society on 3 November 1891.

It was in this period when he also worked as an Army Coach. As such, he helped young men from wealthy families prepare themselves to meet the rigorous standards set by the Army for entry to Sandhurst as a Cadet Army Officer. Several sources mention that he coached Winston Churchill. In 1906, a press report said he had *"fitted nearly 2,000 students for various services'*.

After his father's death in 1898, he looked after his elderly mother who died in 1902. At the time of the 1901 census, he was the Headmaster of Kew College. Shortly after his mother's death, he moved to Bath where he continued his teaching career as 'professor of science and mathematics' at Prior Park alongside continuing his study of theology to fit him for ordination as a Catholic priest. Clifton diocese bought Prior Park in 1830 with a view to its becoming England's first Catholic University but used it as a seminary called the Sacred Heart. This closed in 1856. In 1867, Bishop Clifford converted it into a Grammar school. This closed in 1904. In 1924, the Christian Brothers founded a boys' boarding school in Prior Park. Today it is a co-educational Catholic School for students aged 11 to 18 *'in the Catholic tradition and ecumenical spirit'*.

Priesthood

In January 1904, Thomas Morton left Prior Park to serve at the Holy Cross Church, Bedminster prior to his ordination for Clifton Diocese on Trinity Sunday, 29th May 1904. He remained at Bedminster until September 1905, when he moved to St Nicholas of Tolentino church. In August 1906, Thomas became its Rector (priest in charge) of St Nicholas', one of the oldest and the largest Catholic Churches in Bristol. Its original purpose was to cater for refugees fleeing from the Irish Potato Famine in the 1840s.

The press reported Father Morton's arrival saying:

"Canon Coxon's successor at St. Nicholas, Father T. W. Morton, has been in the parish since October, and has, during that time, won the affection of those who have been under his care. Father Morton is native of Lincolnshire, and he has not been the ministry very long. … He now has the care of the largest Catholic parish in Bristol, there being about 3,000 people of the creed in St. Nicholas. During Canon Coxon's absence last winter, Father Morton had charge of the parish, and there is no doubt from the impression then created, that while the parishioners

will lament their loss by the departure of Canon Coxon, they will feel that they could not have wished for more suitable successor than Father Morton." (Western Daily Press - Thursday 2 August 1906).

Speaking at the event marking Canon Coxon's departure, Father Morton talked about the vocation of a parish priest saying *'the wide world over there is no relationship more tender and striking deeper into the heart, after the relationship of natural family, than the relationship of a parish priest and his people'*. (Western Daily Press - Friday 7 September 1906).

As Rector of the largest parish in Bristol, he attended many events in the diocese to mark clergy retirements, offer support for groups within the church, celebrate school openings or raise funds for various causes. For example in 1910, he attended the special general meeting of the Women's Catholic League in the Clifton diocese that had grown from 85 to 3,000 members in just three years. He also lectured widely on a range of social and economic issues from a Catholic and liberal perspective.

Education lay at the core of his ministry at St Nicholas. He was a leading light in campaigns to ease the financial burdens on parents sending their children to Catholic schools and to ensure the appointment of *'genuinely Catholic teachers'* to its schools. In November 1908, he represented Clifton Diocese (alongside the Bishop, another priest and one layperson) at a special meeting of the Catholic Education Council in Westminster. Following this meeting, the campaign gained momentum and the Government changed its approach on both issues.

His work furthering Catholic education took on a local dimension when the Education Department condemned the old school buildings in St Nicholas parish. He launched ambitious plans for a new 520-place school that would cost £4.500 – over £1m in 2018 prices. Having raised about £1.500 (£400,000), the Bishop laid the foundation stone for the new school in July 1910 and the buildings opened a year later.

In March 1914, the parishioners marked Father Morton's departure for Wells:

"The Rev. Father Morton, who for seven years was Rector of St. Nicholas (R.C.) Parish, Bristol, was the recipient, last night, of a handsome illuminated address and cheque for 30 guineas (about £2,750); the gifts of the members of the congregation. The event took place, quite appropriately, in the new schools, which have been erected chiefly through the strenuous efforts of Father Morton, who left St. Nicholas more than two months ago to take up duties at Wells.

The high esteem which Father Morton was held by the people of St. Nicholas, was demonstrated by the large gathering which assembled last night, and gave him very enthusiastic welcome. The address set out in comprehensive manner the good work which he did When rector. … Mr J. R. Lyons in presenting the illuminated address highlighted Father Morton's service as 'a true priest'; the congregation's gratitude for his labours and deep sense of loss at his departure; and saw his eminence in the practice of all priestly duties. Mr Lyons mentioned specifically his work in connection with the schools highlighting his anxious work collecting funds, the negotiations with the education authorities and his care and patience while acting clerk of the works. He noted that his efforts had been crowned by the erection of the schools as fine and efficient as any found in Bristol. Beyond this was his work in the formation, equipment and leadership of a fine body of Boy Scouts and more widely his frequent popular lectures on various historical and scientific subjects. (Western Daily Press - Tuesday 24 March 1914).

Wells

Within weeks of Father Morton's arrival, he made his presence felt in the City and the broad shape of his ministry began to emerge.

His primary responsibilities were in relation to individual members and families in the city's Catholic Community. Inevitably and rightly, these most important aspects of a Parish Priest's work are private, especially during and immediately after the Great War when so many people and families faced tough and uncertain times.

Equally, paper shortages during the war meant that the Wells Journal, like other papers, curtailed its coverage of many local events marking it difficult to provide a fully rounded picture of Father Morton's ministry during the war. He delivered many lectures for the Workers Educational Association and the Wells Natural History & Archaeological Society (WNHAS). The Wells Journal reported these in detail.

Looking at his work in the round, the main themes in Father Morton's main ministry were:

- Remaining true to the traditions and doctrines of the Catholic Church following the lines confirmed at the First Vatican Council of 1869-70.
- Education and development of young people
- Nurturing the Boy Scout Movement in Wells
- Offering leadership to city institutions including the Wells Wells Natural History and Archaeological Society and the Workers Education Association (WEA)
- Contributing to the City's work to support people displaced by the war
- Stimulating a debate about the nature of a just and lasting peace that would follow the war (reflecting Pope Benedict XV's day of prayer in 1915 and seven-point peace plan in 1917) and the nature of society and economy that would best serve all the people of Britain after the war.

In all these areas, he displayed a liberal minded stance and was not afraid of challenging widely accepted views and policies that did not take forward his ambition for a just and peaceful city within a nation contributing positively to a new world order.

From the press coverage, it becomes clear that Father Morton made great efforts to achieve a 'presence' in the City for the Church and its beliefs.

While most of the reports of his work in the city were serious minded, occasionally, we see elements of his life as a busy, fallible man. A good example came in April 1915 when he, along with several other residents, was summoned to attend the Petty Sessions for 'not having a dog licence'. The Wells Journal said, *"In reviewing the case against the Rev. Father Morton, P.C. Catley stated that on March 30th he saw the Rev. Father in Union-street, and asked him whether he had renewed his licence. He replied. "I called at the Post Office fortnight ago and asked the officials if they would let me know whether or not I had renewed my dog licence, because I am not sure, and I have heard nothing from them." He added, "If I have not renewed the licence I will do once."* The witness added that the licence was renewed thirty-five minutes afterwards. The Mayor in the chair, said in the case of the Rev. Father Morton, *"this gentleman actually went to the Post Office and asked whether had taken out his licence, because was not quite sure. Instead of letting him know, they took the opportunity of handing in his name as a defaulter. That was not right, and it was not justice"*.

Remaining true to Catholic traditions

One of the first opportunities to demonstrate the Catholic traditions to the wider city came on Corpus Christi in June 1914. This Wells Journal's lengthy report included

"The feast of Corpus Christi was duly observed at the Catholic Church on Sunday, when, for the first time, it was celebrated with an al fresco procession to an Altar of Repose erected in the field opposite the Carmelite Convent in Chamberlain-street. The event was unique in as much that in previous years the procession had been confined within the precincts of the church. The inception of a more elaborate and impressive ceremony is due to the Rev, Father Morton, who has recently been appointed priest in charge of the Mission, and it must be exceedingly gratifying to him that the whole the arrangements were carried out so ably and efficiently. …

The altar in church was beautifully decorated with flowers and plants, whilst the Altar of Repose, which had been specially erected by the Boy Scouts under the personal supervision of the Rev. Fr. Morton, was profusely embellished with flowers and foliage plants … The ceremony was very picturesque and impressive, and … watched in a very reverential manner by many spectators. The congregations at the services were very large, many coming from the Cheddar Valley district. (Wells Journal – Friday 19 June 1914)

Family members of about half of the men commemorated on the church's roll of honour took part in this procession just six weeks before the outbreak of war. The Wells Journal carried full coverage of similar events led by Father Morton between 1915 and 1918. In each year, members of families with sons at the front took part in these celebrations.

On 15th October 1914, Father Morton led the celebration of the co-patronal feast of

St. Teresa of Avila (1515-1582) a Carmelite nun, reformer, writer and mystic. The occasion marked the anniversary of her Beatification on 24th April 1614. At the end of the month, the Right Rev. Dr Ambrose (Bishop of the Diocese of Clifton) visited Wells and said the eight o'clock Mass, administered the vows to a novice in the Carmelite Order, and confirmed fifteen candidates - 12 children and 3 adults.

Early in 1915, Father Morton led a large congregation offering a Prayer for Peace, based on the special prayer written in the Vatican and offered in all Catholic Churches across Europe.

Some idea of the demands made upon him comes from his busy schedule for Christmas 1917 that fell on a Tuesday. *"Church of S S Joseph and Teresa. Sunday morning and evening, Rev. T. W. Morton. Christmas Day, services midnight, 8 a.m. and 10 a.m.; also at 4 p.m., preacher Rev. T. W. Morton."* (Wells Journal - Friday 21 December 1917)

Education and personal development

Throughout his tenure as priest in Wells, he was closely associated with the Catholic School in Union Street drawing on his experience as a teacher. Equally, in the summer term of 1917 when the boys at the Blue School went to the swimming baths instead of doing drill, and Father Morton was one of five volunteers who took the Headmaster's place as an instructor. In the following year, he was a judge at the Boys Blue School 4th annual swimming sports day.

Equally, he was interested in adult education, principally through his association with the Workers Educational Association (WEA) and the Wells Natural History and Archaeological Society (WNHAS). In addition to holding various offices in these bodies, he presented regular lectures to both organisations. Initially he spoke about scientific subjects such as heat, light, sound and electricity. The Wells Journal said in describing the autumn 1917 series on *"sound with a special treatment of the science of music' to large audiences* that *the lectures are of considerable educational value and a debt of gratitude is due to Father Morton for his excellent discourses"*. In late 1917 and 1918, his contributions to both organisations reflected his growing focus on the direction of economic, social and political policies, domestically and internationally as the war came to an end.

These lectures were motivated by his underlying belief that *"our aim should to give all as high an education to each person as they were capable of arguing that the limit should set by mental capacity, not by class distinction or economic circumstances."*

In December 1917, Father Morton took part in a WEA social gathering about which the Journal said: *"All found enjoyment in the varied items which made up the informal programme, and several new members were added to the Association before the close of the evening. The night was cold, and at first there was a clustering of shivering mortals round the fire, but this was soon remedied by games suited to the mature physique of the members, yet full of movement and compelling outbursts laughter. ... The events were punctuated by five minutes speeches at intervals. ... In one, Father Morton explained that "workers" meant all who were not idlers, irrespective of class, and that the purpose of the association was 'the education of themselves and other grown-ups. He said that just as wealthy men felt the call to assist their poorer neighbours, ought men of intellectual wealth to feel the call to help the education of those around them. Wells was fortunate in having a number of men with university degrees, and he thought that, if tactfully approached, they would be of great service to the WEA."*

Nurturing the Boy Scout Movement in Wells

Within three months of Father Norton's arrival, he was instrumental in the formation of a new Boy Scout troop. The previous troop based on the Unitarian chapel formed in 1910, had not been successful. The Wells Journal first mentioned the new troop in its report on the Corpus Christi procession of 1914. In the following edition, it said:

"Boy Scouts. — After a lapse of several months, the Boy Scout movement has been revived in Wells, and under several enthusiastic leaders, the boys are learning to become useful in many arts and crafts. On Saturday the Wells second troop, Wookey, Binder and Dulcote, and Horrington attended the Milton Hill baths for instruction in swimming. After the lesson, they marched to the green outside the Bishop's Palace drawbridge, where Col. Leir, Commissioner for the county, made an inspection and complimented the boys on gaining second-class badges. .... Col. Leir also inspected the Wells first troop at the Catholic School on Saturday afternoon; the Rev. Fr. Morton (scoutmaster) was present." (Wells Journal - Friday 26 June 1914)

In May 1915, Father Morton attended the 'Commissioner's Rally' on Whit-Monday along with members of the 1st Wells Troop of Boy Scouts at Ditcheat Priory, 12 miles from Wells. The Wells Journal said:

"The weather was perfect; and it was a happy band of 20 scouts who, as soon after the delivery of the morning papers set some of them free, mounted a waggon kindly lent them by Mr. Francis, of Hembry Wood, Wookey. The good mare was driven by one of the scouts, Jack Spurle. Two of the troop and the Scoutmaster [Father Morton] made the journey on bicycles, keeping in touch with the waggon party at various parts the route.

A short halt was made at Shepton Mallet, and some Belgian refugees living there gave them milk and coffee, a welcome refreshment after the steep ascent to Shepton Mallet. The damaged hand of a woman amongst the refugees was a lesson of the war. She was flying from the Germans with her baby in her arms, when she was shot at. The bullet passed through her hand and the baby's thigh.

After a delightful journey, the troop arrived at Ditcheat Priory, and received a hearty welcome from Colonel Leir. Their den was assigned to them in grove of trees between two lawns, and the task was given them of keeping sentinels to guard the Glastonbury Thorn..." (Wells Journal – Friday 28th May 1915)

In 1917, Father Morton was the official examiner for the 'Pathfinder' competition taken by Wookey Hole Scouts. … *"Cheers were called for Scoutmaster Morton, and the response left doubt as how much the lads appreciated the efforts of the rev. Father."* By then he was chair of the Mid-Somerset Association Scout Association. He made a lasting impression as *"Father Morton's role with the Scout Movement was recalled at a Boy Scouts' Conference for Patrol Leaders' held in Wells in April 1920."*

In May 1918, the Journal said carried an advert for the *"Palace Theatre. There will special attractions on Wednesday, Boy Scouts' Day, when fine four-part picture, "Be Prepared' will be shown at 4 o'clock, and again at 8. The actors are all Boy Scouts, and the film was taken under the direction of Sir Robert Baden Powell. The Rev. Father Morton will present, and will give brief address on the work of the Scouts."*

In October 1918, *"Father Morton was re-elected chairman of the mid-Somerset Association. The retiring secretary remarked that they could not have 'a better chairman than Father Morton. I certain the Scouts love him and respect him, and I am certain they will their best under him. I have heard it from boys in the town, and I know it from what I have seen." Father Morton proposed a vote of thanks to Bishop Reunion for presiding that afternoon and his Lordship and Mrs. Reunion for their hospitality, and the proceedings then terminated."* (Wells Journal)

Offering leadership to many city institutions including the Wells Wells Natural History and Archaeological Society (WNHAS) and the Workers Education Association (WEA)

In February 1915, he attended the annual meeting of the Wells Natural History and Archaeological Society (WNHAS) along with many luminaries from all parts of the City. In proposing that Herbert Ernest Balch (1869 – 1958) for re-election as honorary curator to the Museum, Father Morton said that *whilst he was at Bristol, and long before he had any idea coming to Wells, he had heard of Mr. Balch's reputation an archaeologist. A society which could number amongst its members one who could be the author of a volume such that of 'Wookey Hole: Its Cave and Cave Dwellers,' had a proud distinction.* Father Morton's role in WNHAS was important in his wider ministry in the City.

In February 1918, Father Morton, in his role as Acting Vice-President, took the chair of the WNHAS's AGM. The Wells Journal said *'In addition to the election of the Society's Officers, members heard a "delightful lecture on Certain Ancient Churches in Rome, beautifully illustrated by lantern slides'.* This was given by Dr. George Browne who was Father Morton's predecessor as priest in charge in Wells.

In March and April 1918, WNHAS heard two lectures on 'Early Man'. The Wells Journal said, *"Rev. Father Morton gave part of a very interesting lecture 'Early Man'."*

Another organisation benefiting from Father Morton's contributions was the Workers Educational Association (WEA). In September 1916 the Wells Journal reported that:

"Members of the Wells branch of the WEA spent a most enjoyable time on Saturday afternoon, when an excursion was made to Downside, Father Morton (Acting President) and Miss Kelland (hon. secretary) being with the party. Downside was reached after pleasant motor ride, and the party were conducted to the Crypt, where Father Horne gave a short address. ... Father Gregory then conducted the party over the school, buildings, and Abbey Church, explaining the many points of interest. Tea was afterwards served in the village, and home was reached about 7 o'clock, the members having spent most enjoyable afternoon, the excursion proving the most successful the season."

In October 1917, the Wells Journal reported that *"On Wednesday evening the Rev. T. W. Morton delivered his second lecture on 'The Course of Sound,' at the Boys' Blue School. ... The lectures are of considerable educational value and a debt of gratitude is due to Father Morton for his excellent discourses."*

In April 1918, the Wells Journal reported, *"At Father Morton's concluding lecture to the Workers' Educational Association on Wednesday evening of the two years' course on physical science, a presentation of an address and a purse of money was made him Archdeacon Farrer, President of the Wells Branch. The address Stated: The following list of members of the above branch desire the Rev. Fr. Morton's acceptance of the accompanying purse of money. At the same time they wish to say it represents but a fractional part of their deep appreciation of his intelligent, lucid, and practical lectures on Heat and Light, Sound and Electricity, and their esteem for his great kindness giving his services and doing so much for the advancement of the Association's interest".*

They also reported on the WEA's AGM saying *"... The lectures on Light and Heat resulted in a grant from the Board of Education of £2 10s (around £675 in 2018) and the City Council made a grant of two guineas (around £565). The Rev. Father Morton, who took a practical interest in the welfare of the branch, had acted as science lecturer, and his kindness was warmly appreciated. ... Alderman J A Tate was elected President for the ensuing year. Archdeacon Farrer, Father Morton, Ald. Barnes and Miss Thomas were elected vice-presidents."*

Contributing to the City's effort to support people displaced by the war

On 21st August 1914, the Wells Journal reported on a meeting *to launch the Queen Mary's Appeals saying that the Guildhall was crowded with a large number of ladies on Monday afternoon, when a meeting was held in connection with Queen Mary's appeal for a collection of garments for those who will suffer on account of the war. ... Father Morton, in proposing a vote of thanks to the Mayor for presiding, thanked the Lord Bishop for his address and said we must realise that there was a considerable danger to us all, and although they must hope that the danger might be removed from them we must he prepared. ... He concluded by saying, "those who had spent holidays in Austria or Germany would never feel any bitterness against the German people themselves. In the present crisis, we would see that God could bring good out of evil. ... Let us not lose confidence in God and His mercy and we would see that He could bring good out of even such tremendous evil as this European war".*

On the day the war began, German troops advanced into Belgium displacing some 400,000 people. By October 1914, Father Morton, like Catholic priests across the country, was a leading member of the local committees arranging for the reception of the 140,000 refugees who came to Britain. He was co-signatory of a general appeal to citizens published in the wells Journal saying:

> *Dear Sir: feel sure that the citizens of Wells will glad to hear that arrangements are being made to receive and support three families of Belgian refugees. There is no need to remind people what a debt this country owes to the bravery of Belgium; and all are anxious to do what they can to help these poor homeless people.*
>
> *Accommodation has been offered, but many things are wanted, including furniture. We append below a list of articles needed, and any person, who is willing to supply one or more the undermentioned goods, which need not necessarily be new, asked to send them to Mr. A. J. Clare or Mr. M. Vonberg before mid-day in Saturday.*
>
> *We also appeal for help to maintain these guests, the costs of which will be about 10s a week. For this purpose we ask for weekly subscriptions, guaranteed for six months; feeling sure that there are many people in Wells who will gladly spare from 1d to Is or more a week. All offers of weekly subscriptions should sent to the Secretary soon possible, and subscribers are asked to commence their payments next week.*
>
> *G. W. Wheeler (Mayor of Wells), A. X Clare, M. Vonberg, T. W. Morton, W. E. Hodgson. Hon. Sec. and Treasurer*
>
> *LIST OF ARTICLES NEEDED AT ONCE Wash stands, sets of bedroom ware, crockery for 10 persons, blankets, sheets, pillow cases, two looking-glasses, three door mats, one oil stove for heating, three lamps, three oil cans, three buckets, three tin kettles, three teapots, saucepans, three mops, three dust pans and three large galvanized tubs, three brooms, six candlesticks, knives, forks, spoons, three carving knives and forks, frying pans, towels, tea cloths, house flannels, scrubbing brushes, soap, oil, coal and candles. Any loan of furniture will be acceptable.*

By early 1915 all, the refugees coming to Wells were in housing and some had found work. He continued to minister to around 15 or so Belgian Catholic families in Wells until they left the city. In November the Belgian Flag Day led by the Mayoress resulted in £13 being forwarded to the National Relief Fund for Belgian Refugees – including 14s 6d raised by the Catholic Church. This is about £1,200 and £55 respectively in 2017 prices

At least one of the families, headed by Albert Van Eyken remained in Wells after the Great War living at 2 West Street. He was a tailor and opened his own business in the 1920s. He died in 1929. His family remained in Wells with his children doing well at the Blue School, one becoming its head boy. His son, Alois, matriculated and gained an upper second-class degree from London University in 1937.

Stimulating a developing debate about the nature of a peace that would follow the war both the type of peace settlement that might secure a lasting peace (especially after the Pope's statement about securing a just and peaceful armistice)

On 1 August 1917, Pope Benedict XV issued a seven-point peace plan stating that:

- "the moral force of right ... be substituted for the material force of arms,"
- there must be "simultaneous and reciprocal diminution of armaments,"
- a mechanism for "international arbitration" must be established,
- "true liberty and common Rights over the sea" should exist
- there should be a "renunciation of war indemnities",
- occupied territories should be evacuated, and
- there should be "an examination ... of rival claims"

Great Britain enjoyed good relationships with the Vatican at the time, reacted favourably, although popular opinion was divided. US President Woodrow Wilson rejected the plan. Bulgaria and Austria-Hungary were also favourable, but Germany replied ambiguously. Some of the proposals were eventually included in Woodrow Wilson's Fourteen Points in his call for peace issued in January 1918 and the Treaties that bought the war to an end.

In Europe, each side saw the Pope as biased in favour of the other and was unwilling to accept the terms he proposed. Although initially unsuccessful, the Pope's efforts enhanced papal prestige and served as a model for the peace efforts of Pius XII before and during World War II, the policies of Paul VI during the Vietnam War, and of John Paul II before and during the War in Iraq.

Following hostile coverage of Pope Benedict XV's initiative by the Wells Journal, Father Morton wrote a long open letter to the editor pointing out that it had misrepresented the proposals in many ways, in particular it had:

- raised the spectre of 'papal infallibility' that had been misrepresented in protestant countries since the First Vatican Council in 1870;
- Ignored the Pope's wish for nothing short of a "just and lasting peace"
- The Pope's conclusion that fighting the war out to a conclusion meant that a peace could only be brought about by the "suicide of Europe"
- Invitation to the the belligerents to consider if that "just and lasting peace" secured by mutual agreement

*Stimulating discussion about the nature of society and economy
that would best serve all the people of Britain after the war*

In December 1918, Father Morton in a further WEA lecture entitled "The Family and the State" asked whether "man had a right work simply and solely for his own pleasure without reference to the public good."

He argued that the family was the foundation of national welfare and greatness, the principal source of both virtue and happiness. The family rather than the individual should be the social unit and the basis of civil society. … Inasmuch as the great majority ought to spend practically all their lives in its circle, either as subjects or as heads. Only in the family, could the individual be properly reared, educated and given that formation of character that would make a good man and a good citizen. Joy and sorrow, honour, and disgrace touched the family as a whole, and acted as a spur to good service, and a bridle to evil passions. He concluded by listing of the enemies of the family that he saw as sterilisation by public authority, divorce and restriction of child bearing.

In later lectures in this series, he focused on poverty, poor housing, the role of trades unions and 'the empty recreation ground' – that he described as "The Saddest Sight in Wells".

In these lectures, he said that a Christian would grant that every individual in the human race was made up body and soul linked in the closest natural union. The whole man was destined ultimately to continue his life in a world after this, and his future blessedness consisted in the vision and enjoyment of God. From this, he said, it followed that all men were equal in four respects:

(1) the dignity of their constitution whereby a 'body is wedded to a spiritual and immortal soul;

(2) in their origin, each soul being an immediate creation God;

(3) in their ultimate destiny, which is the everlasting company of God; and

(4) in such essential rights and duties as flow from those primary facts.

Their natural capabilities, which are manifestly unequal, consisted in the powers of body, sense, intellect and will. From this flowed certain inherent rights such as:

(1) the right to live, that is to preserve and defend one's life and maintain it at a human standard;

(2) the right to be educated in religion and moral good conduct, in a fitting measure of secular knowledge, and in some craft or skill gain a livelihood:

(3) the right to labour, both a means self-expression and acquiring the necessities of life;

(4) the right to rest and recreation; and the right to perform duties towards the Creator.

These rights were part of the natural capital of each individual, and neither by his own act nor by the act any other person or society, could they taken from him; save in quite special circumstances by the intervention some higher law, such as the manifest good of the community.

These ideas presented by Father Morton prefigured our modern understanding of Human Rights. A modest step towards 'Human rights' came in the 1919 League of Nations Covenant. Although policy makers drafting the covenant considered provisions promoting rights for minorities, religions, women, and labour; only women's and labour rights were incorporated in the Covenant. During the Second World War, the Allies adopted the Four Freedoms—freedom of speech, freedom of religion, freedom from fear, and freedom from want—as their basic war aims. The United Nations Charter *"reaffirmed faith in fundamental human rights, and dignity and worth of the human person"* and committed all member states to promote *"universal respect for, and observance of, human rights and fundamental freedoms for all without distinction as to race, sex, language, or religion".* These became the framework for action provided by the Universal Declaration of Human Rights in 1948.

Father Morton's ideas underpinned his contribution to the emerging debate on the nature of any memorial in the city to those killed in the war. He advocated the creation of an institute that successive generations could use to develop their knowledge and skills whilst enjoying a wide range of recreations on offer.

Early 1919

At the start of 1919, the Wells Journal resumed a fuller coverage of various aspects of community life. These reports give an insight into the numerous contributions made by Father Morton to the City in the period just after the armistice. The reports mentioned his involvement in:

Boxing Day 1919 Football: "between the 1st Wells Boy Scouts and Stratton Boy Scouts, played the Athletic Ground, the home team being victors 9 goals to 1. … Scoutmaster Father T. W Morton (Wells) and Scoutmaster T. Bailey (Stratton) were interested onlookers at the match". (Wells Journal - Friday 03 January 1919)

A supper for the Wells Volunteers: "… a supper held at the White Hart Hotel, during which the Rev. T. W. Morton proposed a toast to "H.M. Forces". He accorded fitting praise for the magnificent and unconquerable spirit of all branches of the Service, and took the opportunity to solicit help in the promotion of the Boy Scout movement, which he commended as the finest training that had ever been invented for boys. …" Wells Journal (Friday 17 January 1919)

Workers' Educational Association – with details of his lectures mentioned earlier; his participation in a WEA meeting reported in the Wells Journal entitled "A chance for the children - Training the young - The problems of education and suitable work - Play also necessary". Wells Journal - Friday 7 February 1919

Wells Natural History and Archaeological Society – Father Morton provided several lectures on topical issues and was re-elected as one of its vice-presidents (Wells Journal - Friday 14 February 1919).

Catholic School Concert: where at the end of the performance, the Rev. Father Morton, in his usual happy style, voiced the interchange of thanks between the audience and the dramatis personae". (Wells Journal - Friday 28 February 1919)

Tennis Club: A meeting the members this Club was held at the Conservative Club, the Rev. Father Morton took the chair and was subsequently elected as President of the Club." (Wells Journal - Friday 11 April 1919)

Father Morton leaves Wells

The news of his departure from Wells emerged gradually during the course of 1919 through the Wells Journal when it reported:

"At the WEA's annual meeting at the Red Lion Temperance Hotel in May, members heard an apology for absence from Father Morton, who said that had met with accident when in London, which would prevent his return to Wells for some time. He added that the accident was of such a serious nature that they could not expect the reverend gentleman's return to Wells for five or six months." (Wells Journal - Friday 30 May 1919)

"We learn that the Rev. Father T. W. (Morton, the well-known and popular priest of the Catholic Church in Wells, is making slow but sure progress towards recovery. The rev. gentleman, it will be recalled, met with a serious cycling accident some time ago, and is at present in nursing home in Liverpool "(Wells Journal – Friday 8 August 1919)

"SCOUTS' ASSOCIATION. The annual meeting of the- members of the above association was held the Bishop's Palace, Wells. Saturday afternoon. … Throughout the whole proceedings, there was a keen note of regret at the active withdrawal of Father Morton from the work of the Association, of which he was chairman, owing to a very serious accident he met with in London. … The Bishop extended his sympathy to Father Morton and his friends in the very serious accident and consequent suffering, which had fallen upon him. His Lordship proposed that a letter of sympathy written on behalf of the Association and this was carried." (Wells Journal - Friday 31 October 1919)

"Mayor's annual review … A serious accident to Father T. Morton robbed the Catholic Church of the services of a zealous priest, and the city of an ardent worker on behalf of the lads and many institutions in the city. His successor, the Rev. J. Field, has been warmly welcomed." (Wells Journal - Friday 26 December 1919)

Canada

After his accident, Rev Morton convalesced in Liverpool possibly to be close to his brother and nephews, one of whom died in the 1919 Flu epidemic. Once he was well enough he had to consider his future as a new parish priest had taken his place in Wells.

He went to Winnipeg in 1919 to assist in the newly formed Roman Catholic Archdiocese of Winnipeg under the leadership of the Most Reverend Alfred A. Sinnott, D.D who remained its Archbishop until 1952. In the following year, Rev Morton became the rector of St. Mary's Cathedral. He also served as President of the Winnipeg Branch of the Royal Astronomical Society of Canada.

In 1924, the Wells Journal published a long article about his progress in Canada saying:

"Father (later Monsignor) Morton became the rector of St. Mary's Cathedral and devoted much of his time, funds and energy to establishing a children's camp with ornate buildings and gardens beside the western shores of Lake Winnipeg. Many underprivileged Catholic children spent a week of their summer holidays in camp; the boys in July and the girls in August. …

The Northwest Review, the leading Catholic Journal of Western Canada, contains an interesting article on a unique building, designed by the Rev. Father T. W. Morton, who is well remembered in Wells, where for some time he was Priest in charge of the local church. … that castle is Champion Tower. Father Morton built Champion Tower at his own expense and named it after his maternal grandfather who had done some notable architectural work in London. His wish was to provide for himself a home in Canada, impervious to the climate at all seasons, where he could study without interruption, and on occasions entertain a few friends." (Wells Journal – Friday 10 October 1924)

Monsignor Morton retired in 1934 and died in June 1945. Although his death came a quarter of a century after he left Wells, the Wells Journal published an obituary:

"Death of the Rt. Rev. Mgr. Morton FORMERLY IN CHARGE AT WELLS. Many old friends in Wells will regret to hear of the death of the Rt. Rev. Mgr. Thomas W. Morton, who died in Canada, on Tuesday of last week, at the age of 83. An English born prelate, Mgr. Morton was once a tutor to Mr. Winston Churchill. He was a teacher before entering for the priesthood and worked in London for a period as an army coach. Born at Boston, Lincs, Mgr. Morton was the son of an Anglican clergyman who had been received into the Church in 1853 by Cardinal Newman. He was educated at Ince Blundell St. Edward's College, Liverpool, and Stonyhurst and became science master at Beaumont. Ordained in 1904, he served as Rector of St. Nicholas, Bristol, from 1906 to 1913, when he took charge of the church in Wells. He went to Canada six years later and became Rector of the Cathedral parish in Winnipeg, retiring in 1934." (Wells Journal – Friday 06 July 1945)

THE CATHOLIC COMMUNITY
ON THE 'HOME FRONT'

As mentioned previously we do not have an accurate list of the members of the Catholic community in Wells during the Great War. This makes it difficult to understand fully the contribution they made to the wider war effort. Then as now, some people are mentioned frequently in newspapers, for both good and bad reasons, whereas others hardly get a mention. Women in particular attracted much less attention than men did. This is not a comprehensive of the many ways that people contributed to the war effort in the city. Rather it reflects the areas that attracted most attention in the Wells Journal.

WAR RELATED LEGISLATION

The four main pieces of legislation affecting local people during the Great War were:

The National Registration Act 1915 provided for a register of all people between the ages of 15 and 65, who were not members of the Armed Forces. The central registration authority was the Registrar General while local administration was by urban and rural districts in Somerset. Shortly after 15th August 1915, local administrators produced statistical summaries from the forms and issued Identity cards that the public were expected to carry.

The collated figures showed that 1,413,900 men in England and Wales were still available for national service. This persuaded many politicians that conscription should be introduced leading to the Military Service Act 1916 – see below.

The Munitions of War Act 1915 imposed strong regulations on wages, hours and employment conditions making it an offence for a worker to leave his current job in 'Controlled Establishments' without the consent of the employer, which in practice was "almost impossible" to obtain. The Act forbade strikes and lockouts, and replaced them with compulsory arbitration with munitions tribunals to enforce good working practices; suspended restrictive practices by trade unions and and limited labour mobility between jobs. In time, courts widened ruled the definition of munitions to include textile and dockworkers.

The Military Service Act 1916 came into force on 2nd March 1916 and specified that men between 18 and 41 years old were liable to be called up for service in the army unless they were married, widowed with children, serving in the Royal Navy, a minister of religion, or working in one of a number of reserved occupations. Later acts extended liability for military service to married men (May 1916) and raised the age limit to 51 (1918).

Men or their employers who objected to an individual's call-up could apply to a local Military Service Tribunal. These could grant exemption from service, usually conditional or temporary with a right of appeal to a County Appeal Tribunal. These tribunals could insist that the individual concerned enlist, defer entry, or grant an exemption. These tribunals consisted mostly of local representatives from the 'great and good' including women, employers and representatives of organised labour.

There were 2.5 million men in reserved occupations by 1918. The list of reserved occupations published in November 1915 gave the main groups seen as vitally important for war work. It included:

- Occupations required for production or transport of munitions;
- Coal Mining;
- Agricultural Occupations;
- Certain occupations in mining, other than coal;
- 'Railway Servants' employed in the manipulation of traffic and in the maintenance of the lines and rolling stock;
- Other occupations deemed to be 'of cardinal importance' for the maintenance of some other branches of trade and industry;
- Food;
- Clothing manufacture.

The list had a detailed schedule of the occupations covered and this changed as the industrial situation of the country changed, especially after Germany developed an effective naval blockade in 1918.

The tribunals received a 'bad press' as many believed that tribunal members were unduly influenced by the military representatives and biased against those claiming exemption on the grounds of 'conscience'. Those who proved that they were 'conscientious objectors' were directed into work essential for the war effort, often in coal mines.

A J P Taylor (1906 – 1990) the popular historian argued that Lord Northcliffe and Lloyd George, the leaders of the campaign to introduce conscription, reflected the mood of the British people in 1916 saying: *"Popular feeling wanted some dramatic action. The agitation crystallized around the demand for compulsory military service. This was a political gesture, not a response to practical need. The army had more men than it could equip, and voluntary recruitment would more than fill the gap, at any rate until the end of 1916... Instead of unearthing 650,000 slackers, compulsion produced 748,587 new claims to exemption, most of them valid ... In the first six months of conscription the average monthly enlistment was not much above 40,000 - less than half the rate under the voluntary system."*

Appeals on the grounds of conscience attracted much hostile press comment. In reality, only 16,500 claims for exemption were made on these grounds between 1916 and 1918 when compared, for example, to over a million exemptions granted on medical grounds in the final year of the war. Although some questioned the efficiency and reliability of medical boards, these decisions reflected the high levels of physical deprivation in pre-war Britain.

The Defence of the Realm Act (1914 was used in 1918 to introduce food rationing from 7th April, to combat food shortages caused by increasingly effective naval blockades.

Previously 'food wastage' was prohibited, for example by making it illegal to give bread to horses and chickens. People were encouraged to avoid hoarding and impose self-control over their purchases. 'Wartime cookbooks', with recipes using leftovers and rationed food, were popular. They included, for example 'potted cheese' (leftover crumbs of cheese, mixed with mustard and margarine, baked in the oven and served with biscuits or toast) and fish sausages (cooked fish, rice, and breadcrumbs). New products appeared for the first time including dried soup powder, and custard that just needed water adding - the forerunners of instant custard and soup.

'The Win-the-War Cookery Book' carried this message: *'Women of Britain … Our soldiers are beating the Germans on land. Our sailors are beating them on the sea. You can beat them in the larder and the kitchen.'*

In 1918, Britain began rationing to try to make food distribution more equitable. Everyone had a ration book showing how much food he or she could buy covering sugar, meat, flour, butter, margarine and milk. Richer families understood what it was like to be hungry under rationing whereas some of the poorest families found that rationing left them better-fed than before the war. Rationing was introduced progressively starting with meat, butter and margarine (April), Tea (June), Coal and Gas (July), Cereals (July), Cheese (August) and Jam (September). Rationing was abolished progressively between 1919 and 1921.

In what was possibly the most distressing ruling under the act, the maximum permitted opening hours of pubs was cut, beer was watered down and customers were not allowed to buy one another a round of drinks.

VOUNTARY WAR EFFORTS

Many civilians in Wells during the Great War took part in or contributed to voluntary efforts to support the war effort. As only rarely were the names of volunteers and contributors mentioned in the press, so we cannot identify the particular contributions made by the Catholic Community.

From the limited information available, it is apparent that different families varied greatly in the extent to which they contributed on the 'home front'. Many of the names mentioned frequently were people from middle class families. The differences between families were not an indication of their commitment to the 'home front' or Britain's war aims. Rather it reflected the wide differences in socio-economic status of their households in the city. The testimony given by Elizabeth Francis when she appeared before the magistrates for theft in 1917, quoted earlier, illustrates vividly the crisis she faced when her husband died in 1916. These difficulties affected both the income available to make cash contributions to appeals and the time available for volunteering.

In thinking about the situation faced by the women in the immediate families of the men at war, we also need to recognise that many men supported large families. Equally, many women's fears and worries went well beyond their immediate family to include their brothers, fathers, cousins and other male relatives in other parts of the country who may have been involved directly in the war. Understandably, their main concern was to house, feed, clothe and educate their children and to care for aged, incapacitated and other family members.

Cash collections

Numerous funds, some with royal or mayoral patronage, were set up to assist those affected by the war. The Wells Journal records many instances where the Catholic congregation contributed to these public appeals. In a few instances, we can identify direct contributions made by the families of the men at the front. Mostly, these came from the better-off members of the congregation including the Muthu family and others of a similar social status. The Sisters at both convents also gave generously to public collections.

On 11th September 1914, the Wells Journal reported progress with the Mayor's appeal for donations from Wells towards the Prince of Wales' Relief Fund. The fund's purpose was to help the poorer families of men in the services. Recruiting large numbers of men into the forces meant taking away the main breadwinners. Often, their meagre soldiers' pay was only a fraction of the wages they had been earning previously, leaving many families without their heads and living in poverty. The Prince of Wales' message in The Times and major newspapers said, *"At such a moment we all stand by one another, and it is to the heart of the British people that I confidently make this earnest appeal"*. In the first week some £1 million in donations poured in the the Fund (worth about £33m in 2018) and around £5 million during the first year (equivalent to around £165m today). The Fund set the tone of national philanthropic unity of spirit that would continue throughout the War. Wells donated some £256 (£84,000 in 2018) of which £14 (£4,600 in 2018 prices) came from the Catholic Church.

In January 1916, SS Joseph and Teresa's collected £2 15s. 6d (£900 in 2018 prices) for the British Red Cross Fund and £3 14s (£1,215 in 2018 prices) for the Mayor of Wells fund for the starving Belgians. Many other war-related funds received similar collections made by the Catholic Church in Wells throughout the war.

Sewing Circles and similar donations

The women of the Church may well have contributed to the Queen Mary's Needlework Guild Appeal set up in 1914. The London Guild, founded in 1882 provided orphanages with knitted garments. In August 1914, the Guild aimed to collect, sort and redistribute extra clothing items to frontline troops, and to organise the production of various cloth items as required by the War Office. Local items went to troops from local regiments on the front-line and to hospitals. By 1919, the Guild returned to its original role of providing clothing to the poor and orphanages.

On 2nd October 1915, the Wells Journal reported on progress with Queen Mary's Needlework Appeal in Wells. In September, it had received and despatched 135 shirts, 146 night shirts, 26 pairs of pyjamas, 26 helmets, 485 bandages, 154 pairs of socks, 50 pairs of bed socks, 40 'helpless case' shirts, 12 cushions, 48 bed jackets, 166 garments for women and children, 3 packs of cards and 6 pillowcases. These were forwarded to the Red Cross Society headquarters, Mrs. Doidge for the Somerset Artillery, Mrs. Swayne for the Somerset Light Infantry; and to Miss Philpott of Cambridge for recruits. A month later, the list of goods contributed had expanded to include mufflers, dressing gowns, handkerchiefs, belts, kit bags, mittens, gloves, vests, pants, towels, surgical gloves and slippers. The Wells group was organised by Mrs Crosse who was the wife of the Catholic School's Manager. The manager was the councillor who oversaw the running of the school.

In that month she received thanks from Trooper King in France who said: *"the warm things keep us nice and warm and give us energy go through our daily and nightly duty with good spirits."* She had also heard from Privates Oatley, Cardwell and Chappell. Private Chappell, a catholic on the Roll of Honour left the army in January 1916 having served for just nine months. Private Cardwell is probably Alexander Frank Cardwell, aged 25, who was serving with the Army Service Corps, 3rd Mechanical Transport Vehicle Reception Park based at Kempton Park in 1915. It is not clear whether Private Oatley is Private Philip Oatley, Royal Marines, was killed in action at Antwerp in 1915, who lived in St. Thomas Street with his wife and and one child.

MILITARY WAR SERVICE ON THE HOME FRONT

In August 1914, Britain had 247,500 serving troops of the regular army and around 200,000 in the two forms of reserves for men below commissioned rank. The word "reserve" was used in many different ways by the British army of 1914-1918. The Army Reserve, mainly made up of former soldiers liable to recall, was 145,350 strong and the Special Reserve, broadly the part time Territorial Army formed in 1908, had another 64,000 men.

The National Reserves

The National Reserves had been preparing for war for some time before August 1914. In January 1914, a branch of the National Reserve was set up in Wells. The Journal said it would *be "hailed with patriotic pride by a large number of men who have been the Service, whether the Army, Navy, Volunteers, or Territorials. For a long time efforts have been made to obtain official recognition, but for some reason or other, a delay appears to have been caused. Now that Company has been formed—and there was quite a strong muster at the Church parade on Sunday—it is hoped that all who are qualified to join will so. "*

The Reserve Company, (Company H) covering Wells and Glastonbury was created in 1ˢᵗ May 1914. It made good progress in recruiting members. Its commander was Captain A. J. Mawer, previously of the Royal Garrison Artillery. In its first three weeks, it had 102 men of whom 86 were from Wells, against an ambition of 200 members. A month later, the members were parading each week in the Bishop's Barn.

When war was declared, members of the national reserve in Wells were told that, in the event of mobilisation that they would be directed to 4ᵗʰ Battalion, Somerset Light Infantry, North Somerset Yeomanry; 1ˢᵗ and 2ⁿᵈ Field Companies Royal Engineers; and Army Service Corps (ASC).

The ASC undertook tasks that were vital to the war effort but did not usually involve direct engagement with the enemy. They managed the enormously complex task of supplying the resources needed by fighting men using horse and motor vehicles, railways and waterways. At its peak, the ASC numbered 10,547 officers and 315,334 men at home and in every theatre of the war. They made up around 9% of the forces available.

In December 1915, the Wells Journal contained "*a cordial invitation to men to join or train with the Volunteers and listing the advantages of doing so. Namely, (1) it will enable men to get over the irksome recruit stage with a minimum of inconvenience. (2) It will enable them to get into good physical condition and thus facilitate their subsequent training, and prevent any feeling of undue strain when they are called up (3) it will be of great assistance in securing early and rapid promotion when they join the Colours. (4) If numbers permit, men in the same Group will, as far as possible, are trained together, so that when called up they may, if they wish, join the same regiment, and thus retain the esprit de corps of their Volunteer battalion. The subscription to the Corps was one penny per week. Men who are full members of the Corps were entitled the red G.R. brassard and to wear the Corps' uniform. … No expense will be entailed. … All men who wish to join are asked to attend the drills at the Bishop's Barn, Wells, any Tuesday or Thursday, at 8 p.m., on Saturday at 7 p.m.*"

A brassard or armlet is an armband worn as part of military uniform carrying insignia depicting their unit, role or rank.

Somerset Volunteers

As many National Reserve members had been called up during the first two years of was, the Government announced that "*an invitation would be sent to all physically fit men over 17, not engaged in war work or serving in the forces, to join the new volunteer corps organised in each county. The volunteers could only be called out for 'military service if and when it becomes necessary for the purpose repelling the enemy in the event of an invasion being imminent. In the meantime, they would assume responsibility for guarding vulnerable points, water supplies and lines of communication thereby releasing Regular or Tentorial soldiers* who would otherwise have to be employed. *This service was voluntary and unpaid. They paid for their own uniforms and many items of equipment.*" By the middle of the month, a 'Uniform Fund' had been launched in Wells and the Volunteers were meeting each week in the 'Bishop's Barn'.

There are no records available of the members' names and therefore we do not know if any Catholics responded to the invitation. However, a press report from 1918 makes it clear that Kenrick Welsford, was a member, both before and after his regular military service.

In the middle of 1917, the Wells Journal published an appeal for more volunteers from R. Granville Harris. 2nd Lieutenant and Officer Commanding, A Company, 3rd Battalion, Somerset Volunteer Regiment. In this, he emphasised that the Volunteer Force had received official recognition as part of the Regular Army and that the newest pattern rifles and equipment has been made available and there was Government grant for a uniform.

The Wells detachment, averaging 100 men, paraded each week until November 1918. They received fitness and military training took part in ceremonial duties in the City. In addition, from time to time the officers organised 'smoking concerts' or 'dinners at the White Hart' for the men. In January 1918, the Officer Commanding the Detachment spoke at length at one of these events mentioning "*Pte K Welsford (applause), who had done so much, and had lost his right arm in one of the engagements. He was one of their members, and now he was back again, he was still taking an active interest in his old detachment*'.

Two weeks after the armistice, orders were issued reducing the frequency of meetings from one a week to one a fortnight and to instruct all members with a rifle in their possession to return them to the armoury forthwith. A final 'smoker concert was to be held and the final parade took place in March 1919.

NON-MILITARY FORMS OF WAR SERVICE

In addition to the armed forces, there were a number of other ways in which men and women contributed to the war effort. These included:

The Special Constables

Early in September 1914, the Mayor has issued an appeal to citizens to enrol as special constables. At the first "swearing in' thirty men took the oath. Men agreed to work for not more than eight hours a week for six months with the times arranged as to interfere as little as possible with their permanent jobs. The specials got no pay and had no uniform, although cap badges and armbands were provided.

By 11th September 1914, those recruited included K. Welsford, F. Trenchard, J. Welsford and E. G. Welsford. Additionally, W. J. E. Browne, aged 43 and his 2 sons, who had attended the Catholic school, were members. As all were gardeners, it is likely that he knew the Trenchard family. Likewise, Alfred Coggan, aged 48, had three daughters and a son. Two of whom attended the Catholic School taking part in the 'annual entertainments before the war. Alfred was a near neighbour of the Trenchard and Chappell families.

In July 1915, The Somerset Joint Committee for policing considered the best way of filling vacancies in the police force during the war, the following resolution having been forwarded by the Joint Parliamentary Recruiting Committee for the Wells Division. *"That the Standing Joint Committee be respectfully requested to make arrangements to release as many members of the county Police Force as possible for active service with the Army or Navy, and to fill their places temporarily with special constables and others."* The Press were excluded during the discussion, but the following decision arrived at was subsequently communicated to the reporters: *"That not exceeding ten unmarried constables be allowed to enlist in the Army, the selection to left the Chief Constable, who shall give preference to men without dependents and those who will agree not to marry during their Army service. That power was given to fill the places of these men if necessary by calling on police pensioners."*

The duty list for special Constables for February 1916 shows the area covered by each constable. Most of the known Catholics were part of *"Section No. 4. —St. John-street, Southover, South-Street, and Silver-street meeting place- junction of Southover and South-street. Leader, Mr. F. W. Symes, 22, Southover; Sub-leader, Mr. K. Welsford, 1, Muriel-terrace, Alfred street, Messrs. F. Trenchard, 5, Priory-place; W. J. Galley, 1, Somerset Villa; W. J. Welsford, 1, Muriel-terrace, Alfred-street.".* ... *Alfred Coggan was the leader of Section No. 8 covering —Tucker-street, Burcott-road, Ethel-street, and West-street; meeting place G.W.R. Yard entrance. W. J. E. Brown. 10, Priest Row was a member of Section No. 9 covering New-street, Chamberlain-street, Union-street, and Priest Row: meeting place "The Vista.".* In addition to regular patrols, special constables also were required at the police station from time to time. W E J Browne and W J Welsford did so on 4th March and A. Coggan and F. J Francis on 13th March.

In the same month, as the risk of air attack grew, special constables took on two new task. The Wells Journal reported *"Precautions against Air Craft. The Corporation have made an Order that all Public Lamps shall extinguished at 10 p.m. They invite the Residents and Tradespeople so control the lighting of their premises, both inside and outside, to reduce the illumination to minimum. Special attention should 'be given to Skylights effectually shade them, and outside lights should be so shaded to throw as little light as possible upwards. In case an alarm being given, all gaslights should be extinguished at once, and the gas turned off the Meter. People should at once dress, but remain indoors and away from Windows and Doors, as in case of an explosion great danger may ensue from fragments of glass and doors being thrown open.*

The Special Constables will be on duty throughout the City, and any assistance required will be rendered by them. Anyone requiring special protection should apply to a Special Constable to be taken to the Town Hall, where provision will made for many as possible. Residents having Cellars should, where possible, allow their Neighbours access to them upon being so requested.

The alarm will be given by the Buzzer at St. Cuthbert's Mill, giving two short hoots and one long one, twice succession. As these directions are given for the security of the Public, the Corporation hope they will, if necessity arises, be acted upon. G. Weston Wheeler. Mayor. Wells, 25th February 1916.

Wells was not bombed during the Great War. Planes and airships concentrated their efforts on London, the East Coast and Industrial areas. 78 raids by planes and airships resulted in 1,392 deaths and 3,330 injuries.

By the middle of 1916, The Wells Journal 'understood' there was a shortage of special constables for the city, several having been called up including members of the Trenchard and Welsford families. The Journal added, "Here is a chance for the "exempted" to come forward and help.

During 1918, the Somerset Joint Committee for Police spent much time in a long acrimonious debate about whether to recruit women as special constables. Women were part of the regular police force in some parts of the country and worked as special constables elsewhere. In the event, the debate continued without resolution until the end of the war and there were no women special constables in Wells.

The Special Constables remained in being for at least a year after the end of the war. They were asked if they would be willing to remain available for *'service in the city and in other areas in case of civil emergency'*. This became a highly controversial move as the Government were intending to use special constables to counter the effects of the national railway strike towards the end of 1919.

In November 1919, the Wells Journal said *"Tribute to Special Constables. —The Clerk at the Wells County Police Court, on Monday, read circular letter from the Clerk to the Somerset County Council, conveying the extension of the best thanks of the Lord Lieutenant and of the Standing Joint Committee of the County of Somerset, to the special constables throughout the county who had served as such during the war. The Chairman of the Bench (Col. A. Thrale Perkins) asked the Press take notice of the expression"*

Red Cross and the Cedars Hospital

Throughout the war, many people in Wells gave generously to support the Red Cross in its work in Britain and the main theatres of war. Locally its most visible work was its military hospital for wounded soldiers at Cedars House; staffed in large measure by men and women members of the Voluntary Aid Detachments (VAD).

The VAD system started in 1909 involving the Red Cross and Order of St. John. By 1914, there were over 2,500 Voluntary Aid Detachments in Britain with 74,000 members, two-thirds of whom were women and girls. At the start of the war, VAD members offered their service to the war effort. The British Red Cross Association was reluctant to allow civilians in overseas hospitals: not least, because many volunteers were of the middle and upper classes and unaccustomed to hardship and traditional hospital disciplines. The military authorities would not accept VADs at the front line.

In March 1919, the The Bristol Times and Mirror published an appreciative article on the work carried out at the Cedars Hospital in its four years of existence. It said:

"The Cedars Red Cross Hospital is a gentleman's country mansion, delightfully situated in its own grounds in one of the most charming districts in England. Before war broke out a Red Cross detachment was formed for Wells and neighbourhood, and lectures given by Drs. H. W. Allan and C. Hincks and Mrs. Gee, and practical courses were held in first aid and field dressings. All these things were at first looked upon with scornful wonder and supercilious amusement, but were swiftly changed to feelings of gratitude when war broke out. The Wells Blue Schools were, in the summer of 1914, used for lecture rooms and fitted up a temporary hospital. As the scholars were coming back in September, the schools had to be given up and fresh quarters found.

'The Cedars', a fine country house in the North Liberty, was vacant at the time, and its owner, Mr. C. C. Tudway was approached. He readily gave consent to the house being used, and it became known as 'The Cedars Red Cross Hospital, Wells,' and came under the control of the Second Southern General Hospital, Bristol. It opened on February 16th, 1915, and its first patients were a number of men from a company of the ASC, then stationed in Wells.

The first convoy of 20 wounded men from the front arrived at the hospital on July 6th, 1915. The Cedars was first fitted up for the reception and treatment of 30 men, and then for 50, and next for 70, with the addition of 10 at the Cottage Hospital, so that the hospital staff was responsible for 80 men. The numbers at The Cedars were constantly changing; the highest at any one time was 71 in 1917, and the lowest was 18 in August 1918.

The hospital was closed on Wednesday last (22nd March 1919), and of the eight remaining patients two were transferred Hart House Hospital, Burnham, and the other six went Bristol for Medical Boards." During the four years, the hospital was open over 1,100 wounded soldiers have received treatment within its walls, and out of this number only four deaths have occurred, namely, three from pneumonia and one from lockjaw. It might be mentioned, as showing how quickly wounded men were conveyed to Blighty, that during the battle of the Somme men who were wounded on the Monday were in The Cedars Hospital on the Thursday afternoon.

The men came from all fronts —from France, Belgium, Egypt, Salonika, Palestine, German East Africa, and Italy. The hospital has been most excellently staffed, and where all have given, some for the whole four years, so ungrudgingly of their services, it would be invidious to differentiate, but mention must be made some. The Commandant, Mrs. Evan Davies, and the Medical Superintendent, Dr H. W. Allan, have occupied their respective posts from the opening to the closing of the hospital, and their duties have been of a responsible and exacting nature. Occasionally Dr. C. Hincks has been called in. Miss Church was the first quartermaster and Miss Philpot the first lady superintendent; but in January 1916, Miss Philpot resigned, and her duties were taken over Mrs. H. W. Allan. In June 1918, Miss Church gave up her work on leaving Wells, and Mrs. Allan combined the duties of lady superintendent and quartermaster. Miss Clayton, commandant at Glastonbury, assisted Mrs. Evan Davies in her secretarial work, and Mrs. E. A, Crosse carried out the duties of hon. treasurer. There was a staff of nurses and general helpers numbering between 20 and 30, all giving their services.

In addition, this this there was the male VAD detachment under Mr. E. B. Smith as commandant. The members of this detachment arranged for cars to meet the trains bringing the wounded soldiers, and conveyed them the hospital; from their ranks, too, were drawn every night two men who went on duty at the hospital as orderlies, and these men cleaned the grates, brought up the coal, and chopped wood; work which some of them might refuse to at home, but cheerfully did at the hospital.

The social side was not forgotten, and a deep debt of gratitude is due to Mr. and Mrs. Trowbridge, the Misses Simpkins, and others. Mrs. Trowbridge arranged whist drives every Monday evening, Mr. Trowbridge got numerous successful concerts, and the Misses Simpkins arranged whist drives for Wednesdays and gave prizes. The townspeople supplied vegetables and sent other gifts, and newspapers were given free. "The citizens have shown their appreciation of this splendid record of voluntary service making presentations to the commandant. Mrs. Evan Davies. Dr. and Mrs. Allan, Mrs. Crosse, Miss Clayton, and Mr. and Mrs. Trowbridge. The services of Mrs. Lucy Allen, the cook, have also been recognised, and of the nurses three have been awarded the blue stripe for having served 2,688 hours the first year of service, and 2,496 hours in the second, and have also successfully passed tests for nursing. Though the hospital is closed, the nurses have not yet been demobilised. Surely the above record of four years' service is one of which any city might be proud."

Mrs Evan Davies was born Emily Geraldine Harte in 1862, the daughter of a banker living 'above the shop' in the High Street and originally from Ireland. By 1891, the family were living in Chamberlain Street. Later that year, she married Evan Coleman Davies from Newport, Monmouthshire. They had two sons Evan and Edward. Emily was widowed in 1899. Her son, Evan died in the flu outbreak in 1918 and Edward moved to Kenya.

She died on 27th November 1927 and a plaque in St Cuthbert's dedicated to her memory was unveiled by the Countess Waldegrave, President of the Somerset VAD and dedicated by the Vicar. The tablet reads *"In affectionate remembrance of Emily Geraldine Davies, Commandant of VAD. Somerset 20, from 1914 to 1927. She passed away on the 24th day of November. This memorial is erected by the members of the Detachment and those who worked with her at the Cedars Hospital during the Great War, 1914—18."* At the top of the tablet is the VAD badge.

ENDING THE FIGHTING, MAKING PEACE AnD REMEMBRANCE

In reality, the fighting in the Great War ended in five stages:

- The armistice between Russian Soviet Federative Socialist Republic and the Central Powers (Austro-Hungarian Empire, Bulgaria, the German Empire and the Ottoman Empire) signed on 15 December 1917. Apart from a short resumption of fighting' the Treaty of Brest-Litovsk signed on 3 March 1918 ended Russia's involvement in the war.

- The **Armistice of Salonica** (also known as the Armistice of Thessalonica) signed on 29 September 1918 between Bulgaria and the Allied Powers in Thessaloniki.

- The **Armistice of Mudros** concluded on 30 October 1918, ended the hostilities, at noon the next day, in the Middle Eastern theatre between the Ottoman Empire and the World War I Allies.

- The **Armistice of Villa Giusti** ending warfare between Italy and Austria-Hungary on the Italian Front signed on 3 November 1918 in the Villa Giusti, outside Padua in the Veneto and took effect 24 hours later.

- **Armistice of Compiègne** ended fighting on land, sea and air in the Great War between the Allies and Germany at 11 am on 11th November 1918.

In time, these five armistices led to ten separate formal peace treaties. The best known and most important of these for Britain was the Treaty of Versailles signed on 28 June 1919. Three of the others referred specifically to the United States. The final treaty with the newly established Turkish Republic was that of Lausanne singed on 24 July 1923.

For Britain and its Empire, the formal end of the war came through the provisions of the Termination of the Present War (Definition) Act 1918 with respect to Germany on 10 January 1920, Austria on 16 July 1920, Bulgaria on 9 August 1920, Hungary on 26 July 1921 and Turkey on 6 August 1924.

Following the Armistice of Compiègne trust between allies and Germany was in short supply. In December 1918, a special 'Class Z Reserve' was created because of fears that Germany would not accept the terms of any peace treaty. It gave the British Government the ability recall trained men quickly in the event of a resumption of hostilities. The Z Reserve was disbanded on 31 March 1920, nine months after the signing of the Treaty of Versailles.

On 15th November, the Wells Journal published two modest items on the armistice, rather less than a report of an election speech by the sitting MP, saying:

"Belated News of the Armistice. The Mayor was in London on Monday, sent telegram to Alderman Tate, saying, "Armistice signed, tremendous enthusiasm." It was handed to the London postal authorities at 11.25 a.m., but the Deputy Mayor did not receive it until Tuesday morning!"

"END OF THE WAR Surrender of Germany KAISER FLEES TO HOLLAND. The War ended at 11 o'clock Monday. At five in the morning, Germany's representatives signed the Allies' Armistice conditions, and six hours later hostilities ceased. In accepting our terms, Germany has practically surrendered unconditionally. She undertakes to evacuate rot only Belgium, Alsace-Lorraine, and Luxemburg, but also all the countries on the left bank of Rhine, including the great cities of Coble, Dusseldorf, Cologne, Aix-le-Chappelle and Treves. Allied and United States Armies will occupy this territory, which has a population of 6 ½ millions, and comprises the most important industrial districts of Germany, but the work of administration will remain in the hands the local German authorities. Troops of the Allies and the United States will hold the principal crossings of the Rhine and on the eastern bank from the Dutch to the Swiss frontiers. There will a neutral zone six miles in depth.

All German troops in Russia, Rumania, or Turkey are be withdrawn. Germany is to surrender 5.000 guns, 5,000 locomotives, 2,000 aeroplanes, and all her submarines, while her warships are to be disarmed. Our prisoners are to be repatriated immediately without reciprocity. The terms the Armistice are universally accepted as not only giving adequate military protection during the coming Peace Conference, but also convincing evidence the whole world that the task of destroying Prussian militarism has been fulfilled to the letter. Dr. Solf [the German Imperial Foreign Minister] *has sent an appeal President Wilson against the "ruinous conditions" of the Armistice, asserting that they mean starvation for millions. Is is, however, expressly stated the terms of the Armistice that the Allies and America "contemplate the provisioning Germany during the Armistice if it shall be found necessary."*

Following the armistice there were two themes uppermost in the minds of the British people – making the peace and remembering the dead, injured and those who served during the war.

At the beginning of May 1919, the Wells Journal published, a full account of the *'solemn service in the Cathedral on Sunday afternoon in memory had fallen in the war.'* This started with a list of those attending and continued with an account of the Bishop's thoughtful sermon.

"The church was crowded with worshippers come in order to pay tribute the memory of brave and gallant men, and remember in their prayers their loved ones who had made the great sacrifice, and had won "the victors crown in gold'. The Mayor, the City Recorder, the

Aldermen and Councillors were present, also the city officials, the voluntary Fire Brigade, City Magistrates, and P. S. Giblett and P.C. Clark. The Lieutenant of the County (Lord Bath) and Major Kennedy were also present. The Comrades the Great War, 28 in number, paraded in the Market place under Lieut.-Col. Stead, M.C., Captain and Rev. Coode, and Captain and Dr. C. Hincks, M.C., and afterwards marched to the Cathedral. Lieut. W. Bown, O.C. The Wells Company of Volunteers was also present at the service, as were a large number demobilised Army and Navy men.

The service was conducted by the Lord Bishop of the diocese from the great stone pulpit in the nave … the Bishop gave his address from the words in the fourth verse of the first chapter of St. John's first epistle, "This is the victory that overcometh the world, even our faith." His Lordship said:

"We stand here to-day amid memories of the past. We think of those who gave their lives for their country, for the cause of freedom, justice, and honour. Such a death as theirs has been gives the true measure of their worth. Their virtues stand revealed in the valour with which they have sacrificed themselves for their country. We revere the brave dead, and in commemorating them, we honour, and I hope may comfort, those who mourn their loss. To comfort, not commiserate, must our object. For we are not here to fill our minds with sorrow for the events of the past but to rally our forces for the future. … We salute the valiant dead. Whether sailors, soldiers, or airmen, whether chaplains, doctors, or stretcher-bearers, whether nurses or hospital attendants, whether women who did such noble work for others, or men who have laboured in the many arduous and dangerous employments necessary to sustain the men in the fighting line, they alike are worthy of the honour we would do them. Their courage was magnificent, they counted not their lives dear unto themselves, and they have left us their example of comradeship and self-sacrifice.

These splendid virtues are what all need, and should all aim at exhibiting in the new campaign. For of what value were the sufferings of the late war if they do not bring a new world. It would indeed be a new world, if there were brought about a better understanding between rich and poor ,if there were a common aim to secure health and happiness for others and not merely for one's self; if the liberty we seek were not that of wickedness and lust, not that of treading down the class of people to which do not happen to belong, but the lifting of all to higher principles of life, of giving wider opportunities all who have but few advantages, if indeed it were 'The glorious liberty of the children of God.' …

Think for a moment what have gained through the experience of the Great War. Who with sufficient discernment contrasts the unselfish, energetic life of thousands of both men and women of all classes, previously to the war were living selfishly and indifferent to the needs of others, but for the last four years giving their utmost strength and time in working for the benefit of other people—who, I say, will deny the enormous gain this really means. Such unselfishness is in itself both an achievement and an education. They are ready; they are able to do more than they ever did in previous days for other people. They will do it, if only they hear the call, for the one true leader, the Christ. …

If you are in earnest in your desire to follow Christ, begin by giving yourself to His service. Then in your home, in your duties there, or and with your companions, determined only to say and do what you know Christ would approve and you will have made a beginning. Then go further, get someone else to act similarly. You and he or she will help each other. You will find yourself getting closer to the Lord Christ that if you persevere you will daily catch more His spirit and you will win victories for him. Here you will find your comfort. The self–sacrifice of your loved one who fell in the war will, by you, be translated into your share into in the campaign of the Lord Christ campaign against the world, the flesh and the devil …

The hymn 'O God of Trust' and one verse of the National Anthem followed the end of the service. Then the congregation stood for a few moments of silent prayer, and presently the notes of the 'Last Post' echoed through the church, and the Bishop pronounced The Benediction bringing to a close a service of peculiar solemnity.

Making the Peace

The Treaty of Versailles is a long, complicated document, resulting from months of detailed discussions on how to turn the armistice into the Treaty of Versailles signed on 28th June 1919. In reality, the treaty was the outcome of negotiations between the "Big Three": David Lloyd George of Great Britain, Georges Clemenceau of France and Woodrow Wilson of the United States imposed on Germany. In addition to the restrictions on Germany contained in the Armistice of Compiègne it included the confiscation all German colonies; the setting up the League of Nations to mediate disputes between members; and a 'War Guilt Clause". This required Germany to take full responsibility for starting the war and pay reparations, primarily to France and Belgium. Later the reparations were set at £6.6 billion (1920 prices) or around £300 bn. (2018 prices); way beyond Germany's capability to pay back completely.

Several senior British delegates at the Versailles peace conference were deeply unhappy with the provisions in the Treaty. John Maynard Keynes, the leading economist of his generation, resigned from the British delegation following the decision to impose punitive reparation payments on Germany and Austria. His feelings were shared by Archibald Wavell, then a senior British staff officer at Versailles, who said *"After the war to end war, we seem to have been in Paris at making the Peace to end Peace'."* The treaty took force on 10th January 1920. After two decades of economic crisis and political instability, their assessment turned out to be right. Britain and France were again at war with Germany – Austria in September 1939.

Celebrating the Peace

As soon as the treaty had been signed, the Government declared a bank holiday known as 'Peace Day' to celebrate mark the end of the war saying, *"it is desirable that Saturday, the Nineteenth day of July instant, should be observed as a Bank Holiday and Public Holiday throughout the United Kingdom".*

The Wells Journal reported, *"The city was gaily decorated, Friday evening promised well for the following day. Quite early, however, the rains commenced, and save for a brief interval in the morning, continued throughout the day.*

The streets of the city, however, were thronged with people, many visiting the city from those villages where the celebrations had been fixed for a later date. The hymn "Land of Hope and Glory", "Marseillaise", "Hearts of Oak", Land of my Fathers", and "Mine eyes have seen the glory." were taken up the adults and the national song was movingly sung.*

Later, to the strains of "See the Conquering Heroes come," and amidst much enthusiasm, the city's sons who had been taking part in the war, marched in three large platoons, under the command of Lieut.-Col. It. J. Stead, M.C., to a reserved space opposite the large platform, which had been erected immediately in front of the Guildhall. The men had been requested, far as possible, to wear the uniform that they so honourably wore in the stern conflict, now so happily ended. This injunction was very loyally obeyed, and khaki, in the case of both officers and men of the Army and the blue of the officers and sailors of the Navy were very conspicuous. On the breasts of many appeared ribbons telling of acts of heroism, whilst the rainbow splash on numerous tunics told the tale of how early the bulk of the men of Wells went out to fight for King and country. The khaki cloth, too, told in numerous instances where the gallant lads had been, the faded material in case after case suggesting exposure to the burning sun of the East. Many there were too crippled walk, and empty sleeves indicated the price they had paid to do their bit, whilst it would have taxed a statistician to have enumerated the golden bars which adorned the left arms of the lads".

A few moments later upon the flower and flag bedecked platform came the city's representatives, and the scarlet robes of the Mayor and Aldermen, and the mediaeval dresses of the mace–bearers made a picturesque scene. His Worship (Ald. G. W. Wheeler) who wore his golden chain of office, was accompanied the members of the City Council, the Town Clerk, (Mr. E. P. Foster), the Lord Bishop of the Diocese (Dr G. W. Kennion), Canon J. M. Alcock, the Vicar of St. Cuthbert's (the Rev. Preb. H. E. Wake), the Vicar St. Thomas (the Rev. H. F. Severn), the Rev. H. H. Rowley (the minister), the Rev. H. H. Severn (Wesleyan minister), the Rev. Father Field (Roman Catholic Priest) and Col. A. T. Perkins, C.B. Every phase of the city's life, religious, commercial and educational, was represented either on the platform or in the audience. ...

... THE REV. FATHER FIELD expressed pride that he, as a comparative stranger, was honoured to stand upon such platform to join in the extension of a welcome home to the soldiers and sailors who had fought in the Great War. He thoroughly endorsed all that had been beautifully said by the other speakers. It was only a few days previously that they were gathered together to thank God for the great victory which had been vouchsafed to their country, and for the peace that had followed that victory. That day was a day for public rejoicing for the restoration of peace, and of gratitude to the men who had been the instruments in God's hands of achieving the victory that they now enjoyed. They had gathered thank them, although they could never fully do so, because they could not yet thoroughly realise all they owed to these splendid men. They were too near the past to realise all that it meant for their country, and

the whole world. Their country and their native city were proud of them, and they could never sufficiently thank them. They were determined in their sphere and interest that those who had suffered should not have suffered in vain. (Applause).

The National Anthem was feelingly sung. The procession of those who had taken part the unique gathering was then formed, and comprised the following - 3 Bands under the conductorship of Mr. P Loxton, the Mayor and Justices of the Peace, the Bishop, clergy, and ministers, officers and of H.M. Naval, Military, and Air Forces, Volunteer Aid Detachment (ladies' section Evan Davies); Volunteer Aid Detachment (men's section); Central Schools, under Miss Marsh; girls, Central School, under Miss Holland ; girls, St. Thomas Schools, under Mrs. Barker, and Misses King and Squire; girls of the Blue School, under Miss L. A. Thomas; children of the Roman Catholic School, under Mrs. Evens; … Rain had again began to fall, but the processionalists braved the unwelcome showers, and made a tour of the city, via Sadler-street, Chamberlain-street, Portway, St. Cuthbert street, and High-street. Passing through the Palace Eye, the procession proceeded to the Recreation Ground, where a pleasing little ceremony was enacted.

The Mayor, Alderman Wheeler who had led the City through the war retired at the end of 1919. In his final speech, reflecting on 1919 he said, *"A serious accident to Father T. Morton robbed the Catholic Church the services of a zealous priest, and the city of ardent worker on behalf of the lads and many institutions in the city. His successor the Rev. J. Field, has been warmly welcomed."*

Remembrance

Many of the traditions we associate with Armistice Day and Remembrance Sunday date from 1919. The first national commemoration, started with a banquet given by George V in honour of the French President on the evening of the 10th November 1919. A joint commemoration followed in the grounds of Buckingham Palace at 11 o'clock on 11th November 1919; exactly one year after the guns fell silent on the Western Front. At this time, King George V believed that *"the thoughts of everyone may be concentrated on reverent remembrance of the glorious dead".* This evolved into the national Remembrance ceremony held on the second Sunday of November at the Cenotaph in Whitehall to *'commemorate the contribution of British and Commonwealth military and civilian servicemen and women in the two World Wars and later conflicts'.*

Three elements of Remembrance used today date back to the 1920s:

The Exhortation

They shall grow not old, as we that are left grow old:
Age shall not weary them, nor the years condemn.
At the going down of the sun and in the morning
We will remember them.

This is the fourth stanza of the poem 'For the Fallen' by Robert Laurence Binyon (1869-1943) first published in The Times on 21st September 1914; just six weeks after the start of the war. He composed these lines while thinking of friends who died in those early weeks of the war. They came to him as he sat looking out from the cliffs at Pentire Point in Cornwall. Although too old to enlist in military forces, he became a Red Cross medical orderly in 1916.

The wearing of poppies...

...on Armistice Day dates from 1921 but poppies have symbolised sleep, peace, death and resurrection since classical times. Initially, real poppies were worn but these were soon replaced by artificial ones made by former service men and women with disabilities sold on behalf of The Haig Fund and the Royal British Legion.

For many people, the poppies recalled those that bloomed across newly broken ground on the battlefields in Flanders. John McCrae's poem "In Flanders Fields" appeared anonymously in Punch on 8th December 1915 was influential in the adoption of poppies after WW1. The first stanza reads:

> *May 1915:*
> *In Flanders fields the poppies blow*
> *Between the crosses, row on row,*
> *That mark our place; and in the sky*
> *The larks, still bravely singing, fly*
> *Scarce heard amid the guns below.*
> *We are the Dead. Short days ago*
> *We lived, felt dawn, saw sunset glow,*
> *Loved and were loved, and now we lie*
> *In Flanders fields.*

The inspiration for these lines came from the death of Lieutenant Alexis Helmer, 1st Brigade Canadian Field Artillery on 2nd May 1915. He served in the same unit as John McCrae – a military doctor and artillery commander.

McCrae's poem inspired an American academic, Moina Michael, to make and sell red silk poppies in New York. A French woman, Anna Guérin, bought the idea to England. The (Royal) British Legion, formed in 1921, ordered 9 million of these poppies and sold them on 11 November 1921. The poppies sold out almost immediately and raised over £106,000 (around £115m in 2018 values) used to help Great War veterans with employment and housing problems. In 1922, Major George Howson set up the Poppy Factory to employ ex-Servicemen with disabilities. Today, the factory in Richmond and the Legion's warehouse in Aylesford produce millions of poppies each year.

Two- Minutes' silence

The idea of the two minute silence originated in Cape Town where the Mayor instituted it on 14 May 1918 as *'one minute was a time of thanksgiving for those who had returned alive and the the second minute to remember the fallen'*.

Subsequently George V wanted it to become part of the annual Armistice Day services writing that it was due to:

> *The women, who have lost and suffered and borne so much, with whom the thought is ever present;*
>
> *The children that they know to whom they owe their dear fought freedom;*
>
> *The men, and from them, as men;*
>
> *But far and away, above all else, it is due to those who gave their all, sought no recompense, and with whom we can never repay - our Glorious and Immortal Dead.*

It allows time for private reflection while creating a sense of solidarity transcending boundaries of age, race, sex, nationality, class, and religion. The original practice of a respecting a two-minute silence at 11 am on 11th November fell into disuse after the Second World War, to be revived by the Government in 1998 at the behest of the Royal British Legion.

Remembrance Day in Wells in 1919 and 1920

The first two-minute silence in Wells at 11 o'clock on 11th November 1919 was a simple event with no marching, no special services, no bands and no speeches. At 10.55, the Cathedral bell began tolling. At 11.00, all traffic stopped. Shops, offices and factories paused in their work and many stood bareheaded in the streets. No wreaths were laid and no poppies worn.

The 1920 Remembrance Day was a similarly low-key affair although the Journal carried a letter from the Mayor asking the Dean and Chapter of the Cathedral to toll the Great Bell at the Cathedral two minutes before the start of the two-minute silence. It also asked that all 'work and locomotion' in the city to stop for two minutes and expressed his hope that *'motorists will not only stop their vehicles, but also their engines'*.

The Wells War memorial

The design and siting of the City's War Memorial caused prolonged and bitter controversy. Father Morton made known his initial views in a letter to the Wells Journal published on 6th December 1918:

"Dear Sir; Once upon time the famous diver, Tommy Burns, plunged into the Mersey and saved from drowning a well-dressed man who had fallen into the river from the Liverpool landing stage. The rescued man gave him a sixpence. A very correct estimate of 'his life-value', remarked Tommy.

I suppose we grasp the fact that there has been a great war against enemy who planned the dire destruction of national life and liberties, and that our gallant sailors and soldiers' and airmen have saved us from ruin at the cost of their lives, their limbs, their health. We propose put some memorial mark our gratitude. To be worthy our heroes it ought to cost some sacrifice. Naturally, all the churches will have their own tablets, but that not enough. Establish the Cottage Hospital in firm security is an admirable work, but a duty any case, and therefore a mean way showing out gratitude.

A free library and reading room seems me the best proposal. "Hands off the rates" indeed! Can we not as a community rise above street lamps and watercarts and be cheerful in the discharge of some our moral obligations?
Yours truly.
T. W. Morton"

He developed these ideas in the WEA lecture mentioned earlier entitled 'Empty recreation ground – The Saddest Sight in Wells' and secured the general support of the Wells Journal. On 28th March 1919, it reported that

"A MEMORIAL FOR OUR FALLEN HEROES to keep the brave deeds our heroes alive before us, an inspiration to posterity, a duty owe to history in the making. Who of this generation shall never forget, have suffered too acutely. The memorial want has inspiration for all time to keep bright the memory the beloved heroes of our city through the days of the dim and distant future have published in the form of letters from our citizens some capital suggestions the form the proposed memorial should take.

We therefore much commend the Mayor's decision call a meeting of the citizens to hear their voice in the matter. In this way, independent minds acting and reacting on each other will bring their collective force to decide upon the host and most fitting memorial the bravery, courage, and sacrifice of our men. We must not forget that owe our very existence to their sacrifices. We in our turn must pay our debt to their memory.

At this point, we take the liberty of recalling some of the suggestions put forward. The Mayor's idea of having a gun with fixed copper plates bearing the names of men who have fallen is no doubt a very appropriate tribute, but we feel is not a substantial enough appreciation of our gratitude and we ought give more. It is our moral duty so the suggestion of an endowment for the Cottage Hospital is admirable in its way, but surely as have been reminded in one the letters the editor, is already a moral obligation look after the needs of the hospital. Do not need the greatest human sacrifices remind is of this fact.

All suggestions received have merit on their own. hut we fee] sure that most our readers ill with in especially recommending the Rev. T. W. Morton's proposal for free library and reading room. This would not only be a worthy and fitting memorial that is also a useful and much needed boon the city. A brass tablet could inset in one the walls of the reading room hearing all the names of the citizen heroes who have fallen the great cause of justice, liberty, and freedom of humanity. "They will not grow old as we who are left grow old. Their name liveth for ever."

The formal responsibility for the developing plans for the memorial rested with the War Memorial committee reporting to the City Council after consulting the population in a series of 'Town Meetings'. In these debates, the main protagonists were the City Council, the Dean and Chapter of the Cathedral, the British Legion and other ex-servicemen's groups, and the families of those who lost their lives. The War memorial Committee had 36 members including church leaders; initially Father Morton and subsequently Fathers Field and Whittle were active members.

The initial issue considered in the complex controversy over the memorial was about the nature of the memorial – some favoured something of practical value to the city such as new equipment for the cottage hospital; converting the vacant Crown Inn into an Institute and Public Library (Father Morton's suggestion); and turning the athletic field into a well-equipped sports ground. Others preferred a memorial cross in a prominent position as favoured by the families of the dead and ex-servicemen.

The design of the memorial itself became the second cause of disagreement, as the Dean and Chapter insisted that the Cathedral's architect should approve the design – and later by the Dean and Chapter, after their architect had approved of a design they disliked.

The third area of disagreement became the question of including the names of the dead as favoured by the families and ex-servicemen but rejected by the Dean and Chapter.

The next issue and probably the most intractable problem was the siting of the memorial. Three potential venues were suggested – Cathedral Green, the Market Place and St Cuthbert's churchyard. The bereaved families favoured the Cathedral Green but this was unacceptable to the Dean and Chapter; but once it became clear that others strongly favoured this location, the Cathedral accepted the principle but challenged aspects of the detailed design.

By the time of a report from the War Memorial Committee to the full Council in March 1920, the position of the Dean and Chapter was that the proposed memorial was: 'unchristian'; it was out of keeping with the nature of the Cathedral Green and the Cathedral itself; it was likely to place the Dean and Chapter in an awkward situation, their having already refused to allow the the Somerset County War Memorial to be placed on the Green; and they did not have the final say on the siting and design of the memorial.

During the long debate on the Committee's report in March 1920, Councillor Normansell said the behaviour of the Cathedral compared unfavourably with that of the Catholic Church:

"They (Councillors) had all seen in the churches of that [Catholic] faith, candles and images all sorts, and things which perhaps might offend the artistic sense, and yet they were there, and why? Not because the authorities did not realise how inartistic they sometimes were, and how out of keeping with the adornment of the church, but they were permitted because they were placed there by suffering hearts, sorrowing hearts, and grateful hearts, because they desired to make some recognition of their suffering or gladness in the church of their faith. Had the committee gone to the Roman Catholic Church with such a request, did they think for moment it would have been refused (Voices: "Never."), and because, at any rate in that church, the church and its people were close together. Today [the Church of England] was very despondent because its services were not well attended, and because it seemed out of the reach of the people. There in Wells, it had a glorious opportunity to reach the hearts of the people and it spurned the people and refused to have a sacred memorial of their dead upon its Green."

Two months later the Dean and Chapter accepted that the City's memorial might be placed on the Green. A week later they clarified their position saying *"they were prepared to consider a design for the re-erection the great Cross which formerly stood the Cathedral Green; the design prepared the Architect to the Committee in consultation with Sir Charles Nicholson, the Architect of the Cathedral Church."*. There followed a succession of proposals and counter proposals over the following two years that inflamed the situation so that many families and ex-servicemen thought had minimised the impact of the memorial, placed it under trees likely to cause it significant damage, and was an insult to the memory of their dead. Early in 1922, the War Memorial Committee stood down feeling that it could not find a way forward.

The council decided to go ahead with fund raising for the design agreed by a reconstituted Committee should set in hand a public fund raising campaign; and agreed almost 100 names to be included on the memorial. At this point, the Council thought that the Dean and Chapter had agreed to a location on the Cathedral Green but this proved not to be the case. In the event, the Council raised the necessary funds, commissioned the memorial and placed it in St Cuthbert's churchyard. It was unveiled on 15th October 1922. This memorial included three of the four men on the memorial in St Joseph and St Teresa's who died in the war – the other man being from Worle.

In the meantime, the Comrades Club on Broad Street frustrated by the seemingly endless arguments had gone ahead with its own memorial. This was unveiled on 1st July 1922 by Col. A. Thrale Perkins commemorating 89 members of the armed forces who lost their lives including two of the four Catholics who died. Several other monuments appeared in the City during the protracted debate on the City's memorial. These included plaques remembering the employees of the Post Office, employees of St Cuthbert's Paper Mill in Wookey and the Blue Schools recalling former pupils who died in the war.

These included poems and letters from 'the front' submitted by readers to the Wells Journal add to our appreciation of life a century ago. One such item appeared in the middle of the war memorial debate on 10th February 1922 entitled 'They Gave Us All':

Seven years ago a son
Went marching off to fife and drum,
His form was supple, firm and straight:
I watched him from my garden gate.
The bonnie boys went marching past.
For war had come the world to blast.

Seven years ago, the birds sang then,
And fields were ripe for harvesting.
But soon the world in agony
Was stained with blood on land and sea,
And now beneath Heaven's vaulted skies
Somewhere in France my dear son lies.

Men gave their all; they fought and died;
Comrades fell wounded by their side.
Crippled and blinded; weak with pain;
They'll never climb the hills again.
Those bonnie boys who went away,
With brave young hearts and music gay.

Think of those lads so bright and strong,
Who crossed the sea to right the wrong,
When Belgium fought so valiantly;
While women prayed on bended knee:
Oh God look down from Thy pure throne
And make the victory our own.

They saved our England where are they?
What tongue can tell? What lip can say?
We know not where their bodies rest:
But this we know, they did their best.

To save us all from shame and woe
Bravely they fought our cruel foe.
Should we forget their names or story,
'Twould be a stain on Britain's glory.

Frances Mary A. Millard, Wells, Somerset, 4th February 1922

This expresses, amongst other emotions, the anguish of many mothers over the delay to providing a memorial in the City and contained an exhortation to us in succeeding generations not to forget their names or story. I hope this book will help members of the Catholic Community not to 'forget their names or story' as we enter the second century after the end of the Great War.

Frances Millard, the poet, was a single woman aged 66 who had worked as a milliner and dressmaker in the City. She grew up in New Street and Silver Street, was the daughter of Sylvanus (a Post Office messenger) and Mercy Millard. In 1881 she was at Hatherop Castle, Cirencester, Gloucestershire, where she the Lady's Maid in a household with 10 servants looking after a family of seven. By 1911, she was living on St Thomas Street with her 89-year-old father who records his occupation as grocer and an unmarried sister described as a Grocer's assistant. In 1939, she was in one of the city's almshouses. She died in 1943.